National Interests, Morality and International Law

Raino Malnes

National Interests, Morality and International Law

Scandinavian
University Press

Scandinavian University Press (Universitetsforlaget AS),
P.O. Box 2959 Tøyen, N-0608 Oslo, Norway
Fax +47 22 57 53 53

Stockholm office
SCUP, Scandinavian University Press
P.O.Box 3255, S-103 65 Stockholm, Sweden
Fax +46 8 20 99 82

Copenhagen office
Scandinavian University Press AS
P.O.Box 54, DK-1002 København K, Denmark
Fax +45 33 32 05 70

Boston Office
Scandinavian University Press North America
875-81 Massachusetts Avenue, Cambridge MA 02139, USA
Fax +1 617 354 68 75

ISBN 82-00-21968-2

Published with a grant from the Norwegian Research Council

Typeset by typer & tall, Oslo
Printed in Norway by Gjøvik Trykkeri As, Gjøvik

Acknowledgments

While writing this book, I was spurred on by the encouragement and thoughtful criticism of two good friends – Jörgen Hermansson and Knut Midgaard. In addition, helpful comments on the whole or parts of the manuscript have come from Jon Elster, Andreas Føllesdal, Lars Fjell Hansson, Jon Hovi, Aanund Hylland, Bjørn Erik Rasch, Stein Tønnesson and an anonymous referee of the Norwegian Research Council. I am also grateful to the Norwegian Research Council for financial support in publishing the book.

Contents

Introduction 9

1 A Framework of Moral Thinking 11
1 Introduction 11
2 Moral considerations 11
3 The harm principle 13
4 Consequentialist principles 15
5 Special obligations 18
6 Moral deliberation 19
Appendix: Causing harm 21

2 The Moral Basis of National Interests 25
1 Introduction 25
2 The doctrine of *raison d'état* 25
3 The national obligation 28
4 Promises in moral thinking 32
5 Defining national interests 35
6 Conclusion 42

3 The Priority of National Interests 43
1 Introduction 43
2 The thesis of equivalence 44
3 Three theses of non-equivalence 45
4 The rejection of absolute priority 50
5 Non-equivalence and rationality 53
6 Non-equivalence and supererogatory action 56
7 Non-equivalence and moral indeterminacy 60
8 Risky policy 64
9 Conclusion 66

4 Morality and International Law 67
1 Introduction 67
2 An historical retrospect of just war theory 68
3 International law 72
4 From moral principles to legal rules 74

5 The Right of National Self-Defence 79
1 Introduction 79
2 The individual right of self-defence 79
3 National self-defence 82
4 The costs of war 86
5 Killing the innocent 88
6 Conclusion 95

6 War of Defence: Moral Principles and Legal Rules 97
1 Introduction 97
2 National self-defence in contemporary law 97
3 Vattel's argument 100
4 Self-defence and anticipation 104
5 Military retaliation 113
6 Conclusion 117

7 War of Offence: Moral Principles and Legal Rules 119
1 Introduction 119
2 Past injustice and present need 120
3 Humanitarian intervention 126
4 Conclusion 134

Epilogue: Peace or Moral Order? 135

Notes 139

References 145

Index 153

Introduction

How should a state conduct its foreign policy? I raise this question with particular reference to international conflict that involves the use of military force. What follows is largely a study of normative problems in war, but chapters 1–3 have general relevance for the assessment of international conflict behaviour.

When the question of how a state ought to conduct its foreign policy is raised, three answers can be heard: It (i) ought to promote national interests, or (ii) should comply with international law, or (iii) should observe moral principles. The first suggestion is often contrasted to the third. Many of those who espouse an interest-based foreign policy do so in express opposition to those who espouse a policy based on moral considerations, and vice versa. A major conclusion of the argument that follows is that this contrast is false. A government has good moral reasons to give some priority to national interests, although not as much priority as certain proponents of an interest-based policy believe. Another major conclusion is that the relationship between the second and the third answer is more complicated than often thought. Certain rules of international law may have to be violated for moral reasons, yet ought, nonetheless, to remain as they are. The use of force is, in particular, legitimate in many situations in which it is, and should remain, proscribed by international law.

By means of this argument, which integrates interest-based, legal and moral considerations, I hope to put the normative analysis of international conflict on a new track. The book is meant to lay the groundwork for a normative theory of conflict behaviour that combines principles of *raison d'état* with legal standards and ideas of moral philosophy.

One may query the practical relevance of normative assessment of international conflict behaviour. The prospect of influencing foreign policy by way of moral argument and legal judgment is not good. While people are always liable to follow self-interest, this inclination is particularly strong as far as foreign policy is concerned. Adam Smith may not be much off the mark in stating that the "partial spectator is at hand: the impartial one at a great distance" when "two nations are at variance" (Smith [1759] 1976, part III, p. 155). I shall, accordingly, accentuate the relationship between theory and practice – between the philosophical exploration of political issues and the aim of affecting political decisions. The underlying idea is that political philosophy has a dual purpose in both telling right from wrong and influencing actions and institutions in the right direction (Malnes 1992).

In chapter 1, a general framework of moral assessment will be proposed. It juxtaposes different standards of right and wrong, one of which builds on the perspective that Smith thought to be predominant in international relations – the partial point of view. In chapter 2 and chapter 3, this perspective is further explored through a discussion of the idea that national interests should come before all other considerations when political leaders decide on the course of a country's foreign policy. To guard against the risk that normative theory becomes practically irrelevant, the partial point of view must be accorded a proper hearing. Chapter 2 shows that the obligation of leaders to citizens rests on moral principles, contrary to the opinion of those who most of all insist on the importance of national interests – the proponents of *raison d'état*. Chapter 3 denies that such interests always have precedence, but at the same time advances a moderate version of the view that political leaders should be more concerned about the interests of their nation than those of other states and peoples.

The rest of the book deals with normative problems of armed conflict. The closest we come to a moral convention bearing on the use of force among states are principles of *just war*, originally developed by theologians and philosophers and later incorporated in international law. Chapter 4 explains the difference between moral and legal standards for the evaluation of conflict behaviour. It argues that pragmatic considerations come into the picture when we turn from morality to the question of what international law should be like in this area. In chapter 5, the moral basis of a right of national self-defence is sorted out. The legitimacy of defending national lives, sovereignty and territory by means of military force is upheld against different objections. Chapter 6 examines the incorporation of the right of defence in international law. At issue are, on the one hand, a radical challenge against all legal distinctions between just and unjust war, and, on the other hand, proposals for the legalization of anticipatory defence and retaliation in addition to defence against ongoing attacks. Chapter 7 concludes the normative assessment of conflict behaviour by evaluating war of offence: Is it ever legitimate and should it be permitted under international law in any form? On many occasions in chapter 6 and chapter 7, I shall defend normative double standards that yield divergent answers to moral and legal questions of right and wrong. The epilogue winds up the book's argument by providing a general rationale of such standards.

1 A Framework of Moral Thinking

1 Introduction

Questions of right action arise every time there are moral reasons for anyone – an individual, a group, an organization or a state – to do or not to do particular things. This book is about right action in international relations, which is not the kind of activity we are most accustomed to thinking about in moral terms. Some even believe that moral assessment is of dubious relevance with respect to the interaction of states. "Let us face it," George Kennan (1954, p. 36) says, "in most international differences elements of right or wrong, comparable to those that prevail in personal relationships, are – if they exists at all, which is a question – simply not discernible to the outsider." A more common and less extreme view is that personal relationships and international relations raise different moral problems and that normative standards applying to individuals do not apply to states as well. This book, however, starts from the notion that there is coherence in moral thinking so that principles of right and wrong carry over from interpersonal to international relations, and inconsistencies and discontinuities call for special explanation. Even if we are sometimes justified in differentiating normative standards, considerations pertaining to individual conduct lie at the root of political morality.

I begin, accordingly, by outlining a general framework of moral thinking. It readily applies to individual conduct, and my working assumption is that it can be applied to foreign policy as well. Its major elements are briefly sketched in section 2 and elaborated in sections 3–5. Then section 6 sets the stage for substantive discussions by laying out the grammar of moral argument.

2 Moral considerations

The moral point of view is only one among many perspectives on normative problems, and moral reasons provide only one among many guidelines for resolving such problems. When, in particular, people make up their minds about what policy their government ought to adopt, they may be swayed by different considerations – their expectations of how various policies will affect themselves, their family, profession or nation, or by ideological or religious concerns. What, then, distinguishes moral evaluation from other forms of normative assessment? We must take care not to beg important questions by mistaking a substantive moral outlook for the moral point of view as there are divergent and conflicting conceptions of what morality demands. In general, moral assessment can be distinguished by two characteristics: it is comprehensive and other-regarding. First, it takes account of everyone who is affected in a significant manner by actions and institutions. Second, it "relates to us and our actions the demands, needs, claims, desires, and, generally, the lives of other people" (Williams 1985, p. 12).[1] Apart from these characteristics, however, moral assessments diverge. There is even divergence in their conceptions of what gives 'significance' to the practical implications of actions – and, accordingly, in the way they delimit those who are significantly affected by what we do. Moreover, 'affect' refers not just to causal influence, but to every way the situation of someone changes when an act is done rather than omitted.

Many people believe that questions of right action arise only on special occasions, and that "a robust proportion of our actions" falls within a "zone of indifference" where moral considerations can safely be set aside (Fishkin 1982, pp. 22–23). We are, according to this view, normally free to live as we like. Such claims are challenged by those who think that everyone always ought to act in the way which will lead to the best possible state of affairs. This is the *consequentialist* – or more correctly, the *act-consequentialist* – point of view, which implies that moral considerations intrude on every decision people make. One should always try to achieve the best overall results, whether acting as an individual or in some political capacity. Consequentialism may motivate different answers to the question of right action depending on how the goodness of consequences are assessed. An idea that immediately suggests itself, is that things are better the higher the level of *well-being* people generally enjoy. Starting from this idea, *utilitarian* theorists argue that everyone ought to do what maximizes overall well-being. This implies that almost every trivial domestic pursuit, not to speak of larger personal projects, may have to be renounced in favour of philanthropic tasks. No one, of course, thinks like this in everyday life, and few see that as a moral shortcoming, but consequentialist considerations can still be a source of considerable disquiet for people of more complacent outlooks. They constitute one component of the framework of moral thinking to be set out below.

The majority which thinks that moral questions arise only on special occasions also numbers people who define these occasions differently and who disagree about right and wrong. There is, however, general agreement on one thing: the question of right action arises whenever someone faces a choice that involves at least one alternative whose performance would *harm* people. In such a situation, it is always pertinent to ask if one ought to forego the harmful action. Not asking that question is, in most people's view, tantamount to blatant immorality. Hence, considerations of harm are a central component of the argument below.

Its final component consists of obligations that arise out of *personal relationships* between people. If I promise someone to meet him at a certain time and place, I have an obligation to be there as promised even if things taking place after I made my promise make it problematic for me to keep it. And if my mother looks dejected and depressed, I ought to find out what is wrong with her and if there is something I can do to help. Such considerations play a prominent role in everyday thinking about right action, but their exact relationship to other moral concerns is hard to define.

In the rest of this chapter I shall elaborate the three sets of considerations set forth above. They will provide a framework for addressing questions of right action in foreign policy. This framework is not, however, a moral theory, i.e., a complete and rounded argument about the relative importance of different moral concerns. I shall elaborate three sets of considerations without trying to sort out their precise implications or priorities. This is better done in relation to substantive issues. Moreover, a framework of moral thinking is necessarily selective. It does not include everything that might be thought relevant to questions of right action. But I shall try to capture the most prominent considerations of a secular mind steeped in Western moral and political philosophy, and I would be surprised if the argument that follows did not resonate well even outside the Western tradition.

3 The harm principle

Most people agree that it is wrong to harm other people, but the specific implications of this view are not transparent. First, when are people harmed? They certainly are when they are killed, mutilated, raped, tortured or subjected to especially degrading treatment. These are all grave harms that constitute a small sub-set of a wider category that covers much besides, but I shall mostly be taken up with the smaller sub-set. If nothing else is said, "harm" hereafter denotes "grave harm". Second, what is involved in doing harm? If I initiate a process – say, fire a shot – that leads to someone's death, I clearly do harm. In general, harm is done by anyone whose actions *cause* other people's death, mutilation, degradation, etc. This sounds intuitively right, but does not resolve all problems involved in demarcating harmful actions. Defining causation is notoriously difficult, as the appendix to this chapter will illustrate.

Strong moral reasons tell against doing anything that may harm someone who himself harms no one. This is not to say, however, that it is always wrong, all things considered, to do such things. Strong reasons of action can be outweighed by stronger, countervailing considerations. Thus, a person may have to choose between two morally repugnant actions, one of which violates the injunction against harmful conduct while the other has another moral defect. Both actions would be wrong, and it is an open question if the duty not to do harm is the weightiest consideration. Still, it is always wrong to harm a person who himself harms no one even if this may sometimes be done because alternative courses of action are even worse from a moral point of view.[2]

With the last qualification in mind, I see no need to dwell on the justification of the moral injunction against harmful conduct. It comes close (or as close as anything can come) to being an irrefutable premise of moral thinking, and can be stated as follows:

> *The harm principle:* It is always wrong to harm someone who himself harms no one.

The harm principle is a *deontological* principle. The term, deriving from a Greek expression for things that "must be done", indicates that an action is inherently right – or, more commonly, inherently wrong. The implication of deontological principles is that people should keep within certain limits in what they do, however inconvenient, inexpedient or inefficient this may be. These limits may relate to more than harmful conduct. To act untruthfully, ungratefully or untrustworthily is less reprehensible than being a murderer, but there is something inherently wrong about such actions as well.

To say that it is wrong to harm a person who himself harms no one is neither to confirm nor deny that harm may be done to someone who harms another person. The harm principle gives no verdict on what we may call harmful response to harm – an action that is either a reaction to the infliction of harm or an effort to stop potentially harmful conduct before it succeeds in actually doing harm. Four possibilities are worth mentioning: (a) it is wrong to harm anyone; (b) it is permissible to harm an author of harm for reasons of defence; (c) it is permissible to harm an author of harm for reasons of deterrence; (d) it is permissible to harm an author of harm for reasons of retaliation. (a) is, of course, incompatible with each and all of the three remaining possibilities, while every combination of (b), (c) and (d) are conceivable. Moreover, few people who affirm the truth of (c) and/or (d), deny the truth of (b). If anything permits a harmful response to harm, defence does. I shall not, however, discuss the various warrants of harmful conduct in this chapter. They will receive considerable attention in chapters 4–6.

4 Consequentialist principles

When a person faces a choice between two actions, the results of doing one thing rather than another may provide a moral reason why the first thing ought to be done. If so, it is not an aspect of the action as such, but its benign consequences, which recommend it. It should be performed for *consequentialist* reasons. A consequentialist judgment involves "double evaluation" (Smart 1973, p. 14). First, states of affairs are ranked according to goodness as evaluated by some value criterion. Then available actions are graded with a view to finding that which will produce the best possible outcome. Assume that A_1 leads to S_1, and that S_1 is better than any other feasible outcome. Then a consequentialist will have to say that doing A_1 is a moral duty.[3]

Consequentialist evaluation is instrumentalist. It implies that any action, whatever its inherent characteristics, may be right or wrong in a certain situation if its performance or omission in that situation is the only means of realizing a desirable state of affairs. Such evaluations of actions relate only to their causal effects. Thus, consequentialist duties tend to weed out deontological duties and vice versa. If behaviour is judged only by its results, no action is inherently wrong; rightness or wrongness shift with the circumstances. Conversely, deontological duties eliminate options that might recommend themselves from a consequentialist point of view.

If actions are to be judged by their effects, a crucial question is: effects on what? We need a standard of value to determine if consequences are good or bad, and a candidate that immediately comes to mind is human *well-being*. If consequences matter at all, they matter if an action makes someone better or worse off. Indeed, the effect of actions on people's well-being seems of supreme importance from a moral point of view. This is, at any rate, a common assumption, which Thomas Scanlon (1982, p. 108) calls *philosophical utilitarianism* – "the thesis that the only fundamental moral facts are facts about individual well-being".

> It seems evident to people that there is such a fact as individuals' being made better or worse off. Such facts have an obvious motiva-

> tional force; it is quite understandable that people should be moved by them in much the way that they are supposed to be moved by moral considerations. Further, these facts are clearly relevant to morality as we now understand it. Claims about individual well-being are one class of valid starting points for moral argument. But many people find it much harder to see how there could be any other, independent starting-points. (ibid.)

Philosophical utilitarianism is a suggestive thesis,[4] and when actions are later assessed according to their consequences, well-being will be the standard of value. But Scanlon also casts doubt on the status of the harm principle as a deontological principle. He suggests, in effect, that moral judgments about the inherent qualities of certain actions are always reducible to consequentialist evaluation of how these actions affect people's well-being. If, for example, someone says that lying or deception is inherently wrong, he has not got to the heart of the matter.

> There is no problem about recognizing it as a fact that a certain act is, say, an instance of lying or promise breaking. And a utilitarian can acknowledge that such facts as these often have (derivative) moral significance: they are morally significant because of their consequences for individual well-being. The problems ... arise when it is claimed that such acts are wrong in a sense that is not reducible to the fact that they decrease individual well-being. (Scanlon 1982, p. 108)

The problem seems less serious, however, when grave harm, rather than just lies or deceit, enters the picture. Murdering and maltreating people is certainly worse than deceiving them, and bad enough to come under irreducible deontological provisions. When grave harm is done, what appalls is not just the loss of human well-being, but the very action as such. Hence, utilitarian premises are not needed to account for the harm principle; it can stand on its own feet.

Returning to consequentialist considerations, there are different ways of translating these into principles of right action. I shall suggest two such principles in this section, starting with a most demanding one:

> *The strong consequentialist principle:* In a situation of choice, one should always perform the action that brings about the best consequences in terms of well-being.

This principle is ambiguous in crucial respects. How are we to (i) measure well-being, and (ii) derive an aggregate assessment of overall consequences from estimates of how various people fare? As far as (i) is concerned, a distinction is often made between subjective and objective measures of well-being. The former take a person's subjective appreciation of his situation as the test of how he fares. This is sometimes called the *welfarist* interpretation of well-being. It can take account of everything concerning how people find themselves – security of life and limb, the material standard of living and much else, all depending on people's desires and preferences. By contrast, an objective measure of well-being starts from "a criterion that provides a basis for appraisal of a person's level of well-being which is independent of that person's tastes and interests, thus allowing for the possibility that such an appraisal could be correct even though it conflicted with the preferences of the individual in question" (Scanlon 1975, p. 658). Objective measures of well-being refer, for example, to life-expectancy and state of health. The question of how a person fares on these scores hinges on the extent to which his basic needs are being met. From a welfarist perspective, by contrast, needs are important only if people actually accord importance to them.

In what follows, I shall start from a broad, objectivist conception of well-bring that takes many things into account. Personal security obviously matters, as do the physical standard of living and the availability of wider opportunities for living one's life as one wishes. But the strong consequentialist principle will have to be left behind. It demands more than anyone can be expected to fulfil, having an air of unreality about it. This is not, of course, a definite blow to its validity. High demands are not necessarily unreasonable, but there would be little sense in tying the consequentialist element of moral thinking exclusively to a principle that few would even dream of abiding by. Let me therefore adduce a far more lenient rendering of consequentialism:

> *The weak consequentialist principle:* If, in a situation of choice, one alternative brings about considerably better consequences than another in terms of well-being, the former should be chosen before the latter.

The weak consequentialist principle rules out certain options in some situations, but otherwise leaves freedom of action intact. There can be no denying its *prima facie* plausibility. It is, for example, wrong to cause serious distress to a person when acting otherwise would avoid this at much smaller costs to oneself or others.

The harm principle and the weak consequentialist principle differ in many respects, one being that the former entails only *negative* duties to refrain from performing certain actions. Thus, it does not tell people to prevent or assuage the harmful implications of others' conduct, or, for that matter, to alleviate the damage natural calamities may wreck. No positive requirement of minimizing harm is involved; people are culpable only for their sins of commission, not their sins of omission. Consequentialist principles, by contrast, entail both negative and positive duties.[5] But deontological and consequentialist principles share an important characteristic: they are impersonal. An *impersonal* duty is a reason for everyone to act in a certain manner towards anyone who may be affected significantly by what is done. The duty refers only to general characteristics of actions and individuals. Both the harm principle and consequentialist principles entail duties of this kind. Any murderous design directed at any innocent person is wrong, and the adverse effects of any action give reason for concern regardless of whose well-being is at stake. The identities of agents and potential victims do not matter.

5 Special obligations

Impersonal duties are naturally associated with an *impartial* outlook. I am impartial if the way I judge people and deal with them is not influenced by who they are or what special relationship they have to me. This implies that I do not discriminate between people on grounds of personal identity or favour those who are connected to me through, e.g., friendship or kinship. In general, the only legitimate basis for discrimination is difference with respect to general characteristics that appeal to a neutral observer. A case in point is the contrast that the harm principle draws between those who engage in harmful conduct and those who do not. Moral limits on how one may act towards the latter do not necessarily apply to one's behaviour towards authors of harm, and this is discrimination based on general characteristics, which does not violate impartiality.

Some strands of moral thinking approach practical problems from an exclusively impersonal and impartial point of view. Utilitarian theory is a case in point. Thus, R.M. Hare (1979, p. 91) outlines a method of argument that "requires us to pay attention to the satisfaction of the preferences of people … and to pay attention equally to the equal preferences of all those affected". Peter Singer (1979, p. 11) writes in the same vein that ethics "requires us to go beyond 'I' and 'you' to the universal law, the universalizable judgment, the standpoint of the impartial spectator, or whatever we choose to call it". On this view, the only morally relevant characteristic of people is, ultimately, the contents and strengths of their preferences. It does not matter how we are related to them. Preferences of equal intensity carry the same weight when it comes to deciding, for example, whose interest comes first. Discrimination on this score must be based on impartial weighing of purely impersonal considerations. There is no room for *partiality*.[6]

Impartiality requires that I distance myself from self-assumed obligations. The importance I invest in them should be proportional to their importance as judged from the outside, as it were. To attain such distance is mostly difficult, but psychological obstacles do not in themselves invalidate the impartial outlook. Anyway, identifying morality with the impersonal point of view is tantamount to denying the moral importance of many special commitments that play a central role in everyday life. They engender personal requirements to act in specific ways towards particular people, and contrast to the universal and impersonal duties that spring from deontological and consequentialist principles. The term *special obligation* is a common label for such requirements. In this book, we will be concerned only with *self-assumed* obligations. They derive from the deliberate creation of moral bounds between people, presupposing explicit or implicit pledges by one person to behave in a certain way towards another. A promise is the paradigm example.

The existence of special obligations is a contingent matter. Thus, I have a commitment of fidelity to my promises only if I have promised something. By contrast, deontological and consequentialist considerations lie with me whether I like it or not. They represent standing demands on my life. This distinguishes universal from particular considerations. Moreover, deontological and consequentialist duties refer to attributes that always and everywhere recommend the actions having these attributes. By contrast, the claim that an agent is morally required to meet an obligation he has deliberately undertaken, is not grounded in features of the action or its consequences. I may, e.g., promise things that in themselves are neither good nor bad, like meeting a friend at the pub, and my obligation derives from the promise as such, not from the nature of what I promised to do. True, people often bind themselves to do things that are inherently valuable, like doctors when they take their professional oath, but the self-assumed obligation still provides an additional moral spur over and above the intrinsic value of the undertaking. So, at any rate, runs the conventional view of promises, which will be elaborated in chapter 2.

6 Moral deliberation

I have presented three sets of moral considerations that enter into the subsequent discussion of how governments ought to conduct their foreign policies. How do these considerations compare to one another in terms of normative force? How strong is, for example, the duty not to do harm as compared to potentially conflicting consequentialist considerations? I shall not try to answer this question in general terms, but rather discuss it in relation to substantive issues of foreign policy. To prepare for these discussions, a brief excursion on the grammar of moral argument will be useful.

Three types of moral judgment will be distinguished. First, certain judgments state *prima facie* reasons to act in specific ways. These are reasons that immediately appeal to us, but may, on closer scrutiny, prove irrelevant or insignificant. One might, for example, think of intellectual or artistic merit as something that makes people worthy of special respect, but subsequently retract this as a baseless (if understandable) prejudice. Or one may hint, tentatively, that each person should take responsibility for his own health and proceed to affirm this demand with confidence. In both cases, a *prima facie* reason is invoked; the first withers on second thoughts, while the second is sustained.

Second, some reasons *are* evidently relevant to the determination of right and wrong. They should be taken into account, but there is still a chance that they will be overridden by other, equally legitimate considerations. The requirement that promises should be kept is a case in point. Most people believe that a promise is always a relevant reason for action, but concede that other urgent concerns sometimes weigh it down. Thus, I should not leave victims of an accident unattended just to be in time for a business appointment. A promise is, one may say, a *pro tanto* reason of action: it should be observed for what it is worth, and it is definitely worth something.[7]

The fact that an action would violate a promise counts against its performance, but it is not necessarily a *conclusive* consideration. But it would be if it carried sufficient weight to override other relevant considerations. While *prima facie* and *pro tanto* reasons are provisional premises or preliminary steps in deliberation, conclusive reasons tell us what, all things considered, ought to be done. If, for example, I am on my way to a business appointment and hear someone cry for help, I have a conclusive reason to find out what is wrong even if I will then be late for the appointment.

What was said about the harm principle earlier in this chapter implies that it is a *pro tanto* reason of action. It must always be taken into account, but this does not imply that it is decisive whenever it applies. Nothing I have said above excludes that other considerations sometimes outweigh the principle that one must never harm an innocent person – nor, for that matter, have I ruled out the possibility that it is an absolute principle that everyone always has an overriding duty to observe.

The previous paragraphs portray moral thinking as rational and systematic. Is it? Can moral problems be sorted out by way of philosophical argument? From one point of view, beliefs about right and wrong are feelings rather than cognitive states of mind. The assumption is, as Henry Sidgwick ([1907] 1981, p. 27) says, that the "subjective fact of my approbation" is all there is to my belief that some action or arrangement is as it ought to be. If someone asks me why I believe what I do, I can "content myself with affirming the existence of such feelings in my mind". Sidgwick, for one, does not see things this way. He avows that feelings are only half the story: "The peculiar emotion of moral approbation is ... inseparably bound up with the conviction, explicit or implicit, that the conduct approved is 'really' right" (ibid.). If so, judgments of right and wrong involve rational reasoning and critical reflection; hence, the role of philosophy in moral and political life.[8]

But even if we grant that judgments of right and wrong involve rational reasoning, there may be limits to how far moral problems can be resolved by way of philosophical analysis. This is partly due to the undeniable role of emotion in undermining critical reflection and weakening its motivational force, but the limits are also partly integral to philosophy. On this score, particular interest pertains to what we may call the problem of *indeterminacy*. It arises if the principles and considerations that bear on a particular problem cannot be balanced to reach a conclusive answer as to what should be done. This is sometimes called a *moral dilemma*: a confrontation of urgent but irreconcilable reasons of action. In the following pages, I shall frequently return to this particular impasse of moral thinking.

Appendix: Causing harm

In section 3, 'doing harm' was defined as doing something that *causes* harm to someone. This definition raises at least three problems that deserve mentioning.

First, it is not easy to tell what it takes for an event to be the cause of another. There are many plausible accounts of causation, but no definitive one. J.L. Mackie (1975) suggests, for example, that a cause is typically one among several factors which together suffice to bring about a certain effect. When we say that an electric short-circuit at a certain place set a house on fire, we do not mean that the short circuit was a necessary condition of the fire (which may also have been caused by, say, the overturning of a lighted oil stove), nor do we claim that it was in itself sufficient (as the short-circuit would have been inconsequential had there been no inflammable material near by); rather, the short-circuit caused the fire in the sense that it was "an indispensable part of a complex sufficient (but not necessary) condition of the fire", and a cause is accordingly defined as "an insufficient but necessary part of a condition which is itself unnecessary but sufficient for the result" (Mackie 1975, p. 16; italics deleted). This definition captures essential aspects of what we mean by causation. It implies, in particular, that I cause harm whenever an action of mine enters into a series of events which produces harmful effects that had not taken place if I had acted otherwise.

A second question is if I cause harm even when an *omission* of mine is an indispensable part of a harmful process. We are here talking about negative causation. The point is that I refrain from doing an action whose performance is a necessary condition of halting a harmful process. In general, an event is a negative cause of a certain outcome if (i) this event did not take place, and (ii) the outcome would not have come about the way it did if the event had taken place. Can the non-occurrence of an event really be said to cause anything at all? Is, in particular, a person who does not initiate or actively contribute to a harmful process, but just allows it to run its course, exercising causal influence on this process? Consider three cases of this kind. (1) I silently watch you walk on to a bridge that I know to be unsafe. As I expect, the bridge collapses and you fall into the river below. Do I harm you by failing to prevent the accident? (2) I passively watch while you float unconsciously down the river to a certain death. Do I harm you by not jumping in to save you? (3) I am not present at the place of your accident, although I should have been. The municipality has hired me to warn people not to cross the unsafe bridge, and I have regularly done so, but this morning I stayed at home without noticing anyone. Do I harm you by my negligence?

In each case, my failure to do certain things is a negative cause of a harmful outcome. But is harm done in any (or all) of these cases? Perhaps the strongest candidate for an affirmative answer is (3), where I deliberately step out of a process whose course and outcome normally depends on my active role in it. Things may stand differently with respect to (1) and (2). Some will presumably say that my failure to prevent harm in these cases is just that: a failure to exercise causal influence. More generally, a non-event which does not consist in the non-occurrence of some regular, predictable state of affairs, is not a cause of anything. It makes no observable difference to the world, but affects it only counterfactually, through people's imagination of how things would have been if suddenly something had happened that did not take place and was not "programmed" to do so. This does not mean, of course, that what I do in cases (1) and (2) is all right. Not to prevent harm is not necessarily less wrong than doing harm, especially if preventive efforts cost nothing, as in case (1). But we are arguably speaking about different types of action, which should be kept apart analytically although they are sometimes on a par from a moral point of view.

After conceptual questions pertaining to causal relationships have been sorted out, an empirical problem remains. It will be difficult in many cases to establish that a causal connection exists between a specific action and a certain occurrence of harm. This problem may seem daunting when we turn from fairly simple interpersonal affairs to complex relationships involving big organizations or states. Consider, for example, the argument that "the transformation to a modern economy ... erodes traditional means of livelihood for the rural population of the developing nations". This is asserted by Judith Lichtenberg (1981, p. 91), who infers that "many (perhaps a majority) of those in the developing nations are absolutely harmed by relations with advanced countries". She readily concedes, however, that it will be very difficult to describe the causal processes more precisely. "Only a misguided faith in the powers of measurement or an underestimation of the extent of international interdependence could lead one to think that these issues can be settled with great precision" (ibid.).

2 The Moral Basis of National Interests

1 Introduction

It is widely believed that a government should do what is best for national citizens. This idea lies at the root of the doctrine of *raison d'état*, also known as *Realpolitik* and *reason of state*. I shall elaborate and examine this doctrine in chapters 2 and 3.

Section 2 of this chapter presents the basic postulates of *raison d'état*, starting with the idea that a government, as the trustee of national citizens, has an obligation to promote national interests, and concluding with the postulate that this obligation comes before all other considerations in foreign policy. Section 3 begins an argument that will lead to a less extreme theory of political trusteeship. The basic assumption is that the obligation to promote national interests rests on moral considerations, contrary to what proponents of *raison d'état* think. It is, more specifically, modelled on a promise. Section 4 explains how promises enter into moral assessment and sets the stage for examining the relationship between the national obligation and other moral considerations. This examination will be undertaken in the next chapter, after section 5 of the present chapter has explained what particular interests the term "national interests" refers to.

2 The doctrine of *raison d'état*

I shall begin by setting out the basic assumptions of the doctrine of *raison d'état*. One of its most eloquent advocates is the diplomat and historian George Kennan, who writes:

> Government is an agent, not a principal. Its primary obligation is to the *interests* of the national society it represents, not to the moral impulses that individual elements of that society may experience. No more than the attorney *vis-à-vis* the client, or the doctor *vis-à-vis* the patient, can government attempt to insert itself into the conscience of those whose interests it represents.
>
> Let me explain. The interests of the national society for which

> government has to concern itself are basically those of its military security, the integrity of its political life and the well-being of its people. These needs have no moral quality. They arise from the very existence of the national state in question and from the status of the national sovereignty it enjoys. They are the unavoidable necessities of a national existence and therefore not subject to classification as either "good" or "bad". They may be questioned from a detached philosophic point of view. But the government of the sovereign state cannot make such judgments. When it accepts the responsibilities of governing, implicit in that acceptance is the assumption that it is right that the state should be sovereign, that the integrity of its political life should be assured, that its people should enjoy the blessings of military security, material prosperity and a reasonable opportunity for, as the Declaration of Independence put it, the pursuit of happiness. For these assumptions the government needs no moral justification, nor need it accept any moral reproach for acting on the basis of them. (Kennan 1985/86, p. 206)[9]

Several assumptions are contained in this passage. In the first place, Kennan characterizes the government as a *trustee*. His whole argument is an elaboration of the normative limits that this role allegedly sets to political action. Trusteeship is a relation between an agent and a principal. The former trusts some or all of his interests to the care of the latter, who is obligated to promote these interests. This description applies especially to the relationship between political leaders and citizens in democratic states.

The second assumption of Kennan's argument is that three kinds of national interest have particular urgency: military security, political integrity and economic prosperity. These are a government's most important objectives. Kennan calls them "the unavoidable necessities of national existence", which suggests that they are prerequisites of realizing any national interest whatsoever. I shall look closer at this assumption in section 5.

In the third place, Kennan stresses that political leaders must not take their guidance from the moral ideas of citizens. This means two things. First, political leaders must stay aloof from "moral impulses that individual elements of … society may experience". They should not let themselves be swayed by groups of citizens who are strongly committed to particular values or causes. Such partisan commitments cannot be allowed to determine the course of foreign policy. Secondly, the government should not "insert itself into the conscience" of society as a whole. The most obvious implication of this idea is that political leaders must not impute moral attitudes or motives to citizens, nor, *a fortiori*, act on the basis of such imputed motives.

In the fourth place, Kennan makes several comments on the nature and justification of the normative requirements that go with political trusteeship. He says that the national interests of security, integrity and well-being "have no moral quality". Their fulfillment are neither good nor bad, and the government "needs no moral justification" for furthering them. This suggests that the requirements of political trusteeship are not moral requirements and do not owe their normative force to moral considerations. Kennan contrasts morality and the principles of political leadership, and other advocates and analysts of *raison d'état* have done the same. Thus, Richard Sterling (1965, p. 260) distinguishes between, on the one hand, actions that fall within "the realm of principle where morality … [is] the commanding consideration", and, on the other hand, "conduct guided by ... no other criterion than the welfare of the state". He says that the "ideal" of politics informed by *raison d'état* "runs directly counter to the concept of a universal moral law which claims for itself the function of ultimate yardstick for human conduct: acts must be judged finally by the generally accepted canons of good and evil and not according to their utility to the state" (ibid.). Robert C. Good (1965, p. 283) is more terse: "The practitioner of *Realpolitik* insists that the necessities of states leave no room for moral choice and that accordingly the statesman must be willing to act counter to his moral preferences." This is in line with Hans Morgenthau's (1951, p. 35) assertion that "a foreign policy guided by universal moral principles, by definition relegating the national interest to the background, is under contemporary conditions of foreign policy and warfare a policy of national suicide, actual or potential". The room for moral choice is thought to be restricted by the high costs of balancing security against other considerations. The penalty one may pay for taking an interest in the interests of other states lies behind the alleged "moral inferiority of international politics" (Hoffmann, 1981, p. 23). Winston Churchill may have had the same contrast between moral considerations and national interests in mind when he said that the "Sermon on the Mount is the last word in Christian ethics. … Still, it is not on those terms that Ministers assume their responsibilities of guiding states" (quoted in Schlesinger 1972, p. 24).[10]

In the fifth place, Kennan does not just distinguish the principles of political leadership from moral considerations; he also holds that the former always have priority from a normative point of view. A government need not "accept any moral reproach for acting on the basis of them"; national interests take precedence over all other considerations in the conduct of foreign policy. This idea is the most conspicuous element of the doctrine of *raison d'état*. It has two implications. First, political leaders should never let personal objectives into their political deliberations. They must place the interests of their principal – national citizens – before private interests. Second, and much more controversially, political leaders should always see to it that things go as well as possible for national citizens, regardless of how the policies they pursue affect other states and peoples.

When I speak of the doctrine of *raison d'état* below, I have Kennan's five assumptions in mind. It will be convenient to restate them more briefly in three postulates:

(1) As a trustee of national citizens, a government is bound by the *national obligation*, which says that every government ought to promote national interests.

(2) The national obligation does not rest upon moral considerations.

(3) The national obligation has absolute priority with respect to political decisions that bear on military security, national integrity and economic prosperity.

Postulates (1) and (2) will be examined in this chapter, while postulate (3) is deferred to chapter 3.

3 The national obligation

The national obligation, which says that every government ought to promote national interests, is a *positional* duty. Positional duties are grounded in rules or expectations that pertain to specific roles or functions. An example is the duty of a treasurer to keep an account of expenses. In general, "positional duties ... are tasks or performances which are intimately connected with some particular office, station, or role which an individual can fill" (Simmons 1979, p. 12).

> This role may be part of an institutional framework, but it need not be. Thus, we speak of the duties of a citizen, a teacher, or the president, but also of the duties of a father. ... An individual comes to have a positional duty only by filling the position to which it is tied, and thereby coming to have certain performances expected or required of him within the scheme in question (be it institutional, familial, or whatever). When applying for a job, for instance, we are told what our duties will be if we take the job, and these duties can be called "the duties of an X", where "X" is the name of the job in question. (Ibid., pp. 12–13)

Positional duties exist in so far as social expectations direct themselves to persons who stand in specific contractual or emotional relations to other people. A positional duty is, accordingly, defined by reference to the occupation of a *role*. Some roles, like daughter or son, belong to a person whether he likes it or not, while others belong only to those who deliberately enter into them. In the latter case, the attendant positional duties are self-imposed. This goes, in particular, for the duties of those who accept political office or become employed as public functionaries. When they deliberately enter into these positions, they countenance that certain performances will be expected of them within an institutional scheme. Moreover, their positional duties involve *responsibility*. To be responsible for something is, generally speaking, to be liable to be called to account for it. As we are accountable for the discharge of all our duties, each of them constitutes, in a sense, a responsibility. But the notion is also used in a more restricted sense. We say that a relationship of responsibility exists between two agents if (at least) one of them owes the other care, concern or assistance. This is exactly the kind of relationship a government is thought to have to national citizens when it is seen as their trustee. Besides, the concept of responsibility seems "best reserved for required tasks which involve some independent planning and nonroutine performance" (Simmons 1979, p. 13). The tasks that go with the conduct of foreign policy are certainly like this. They cannot conform to routine, but involve considerable discretion in planning and performance.

The national obligation may be seen as a positional duty deriving from social expectations of the kind that direct themselves against a trustee who has given other people reason to believe that he will protect and promote their interests. It is one thing, however, to depict the national obligation as a positional duty, and another thing to explain why it ought to be fulfilled. Whence comes its normative force? According to postulate (2), it does *not* come from moral considerations. The doctrine of *raison d'état* says that those who accept political responsibility need no moral justification for discharging it; nor, presumably, does its acceptance provide such justification. Political leaders are obligated to further certain interests, but these interests have, in Kennan's words, "no moral quality". While he offers no justification of postulate (2), I suspect that he and other proponents of *raison d'état* deny that positional duties constitute moral duties, because they conceive of all moral considerations as *impersonal* reasons of action. Such an idea would, at any rate, make good sense of postulate (2).

As defined in chapter 1, an impersonal reason is a reason for everyone to act in a certain manner towards all who may be affected significantly by what is done. It refers only to general characteristics of actions and individuals. Thus, any murderous acts directed at any innocent person is immoral, and there is a duty to assuage acute pain regardless of whose well-being is at stake. The identities of agents, victims and beneficiaries do not matter. Impersonal duties are the only moral considerations that are compatible with an impartial outlook, i.e., a propensity to judge and act towards people without regard to who they are or how they are related to oneself, discriminating between persons only on grounds of general characteristics, such as needs and vulnerability to harm. By contrast, contractual ties that ground positional duties have a pronounced personal character. They involve special relationships between specific people and are a source of partiality in attitudes and actions. If, therefore, impersonal and impartial duties were exhaustive of moral considerations, the national obligation would not be a moral obligation, and I believe, as I said, that those who deny its moral status do so for just this reason. Thus, when Robert Sterling contrasts national interests to the "universal moral law", he seems to associate this law with broad, impersonal demands of a deontological and consequentialist nature. When, moreover, Kennan says that national integrity and prosperity are "needs" that have "no moral quality", he apparently suggests that such quality resides only in universally valuable states of affairs. If, however, morality encompasses even personal and partial reasons of action, then positional duties in general, and the national obligation in particular, may well have moral status. They may, more specifically, fall into the category of *special obligations*, which is where I believe they belong.

In chapter 1, I talked about special obligations that derive from self-assumed commitments to behave in specific ways towards particular people. The positional duty of political leaders is such an obligation. Political leaders become bound by this duty by entering into certain roles. Doing so is tantamount to informing other people of one's intention to conduct oneself as expected of the occupants of these roles. The crux is, accordingly, a *promise*, which is the paradigmatic example of a self-assumed, special obligation. For a closer look at the underlying idea, it will be useful to consider professional roles.

> [T]aking on a role is sometimes appropriately viewed as a kind of promising. The process of assuming a professional role often illustrates this. Many professional groups have rituals of initiation that include oaths of allegiance. The Hippocratic Oath is only the most famous example. (Veatch 1981, p. 84)

The last sentence alludes to the professional role of physician. There exist both formal statements and informal conceptions of the tasks incumbent on someone who practices this profession. They amount to a fairly precise code of conduct, and it makes good sense to say that a practitioner promises conformity to this code. If he ignores it – if, say, he witnesses an accident but does not offer medical assistance – his behaviour constitutes breach of trust. The same can be said of a lawyer who fails to present his client's case in the most favourable light. The legal profession nurtures fairly precise expectations of proper conduct, and those who practice law promise to behave accordingly. Yet, entering into a role is not the paradigmatic way of making a promise. A promise typically creates a new and unique relationship between promisor and promisee. It gives rise to a bond of trust that is shaped entirely at the discretion of the persons involved. As far as roles are concerned, however, the bond between promisor and promisee is ready-made and cannot be rearranged at will. It is defined by the social expectations that attach to the role. Still, the two species of promising share a significant characteristic. In both cases, a previously uncommitted person deliberately commits himself to certain actions and informs other people of his intention on this score.

This analysis of professional duties can be carried over to the positional duty that underlies the national obligation. At the least, the analysis applies to the roles of political leaders in democratic states. Democracy instills trust that the government will look after the interests of citizens. The process of open political debate and free, periodic elections gives effect to this presumption. Laws, institutions and conventions foster social expectations that those who enter into governmental positions pledge themselves to obey. In some states, with respect to some positions of authority, this pledge is confirmed by formal oaths. But even where it finds expression only in informal conceptions and constitutional practice, its reality is undeniable. As, moreover, public functionaries are supposed to be loyal servants of the political leadership, the positional duties of the two groups are essentially the same. This constitutes, in effect, a moral interpretation of the national obligation. It depicts it as a promise, creating the same kind of bond between government and citizens that generally exists between a promisor and a promisee. There are certainly many differences between an everyday promise and the pledge one takes by entering into a politically defined role, but in both cases a relationship of trust arises through a person's voluntary commitment to fulfill the expectations he instills in other people.

To conclude, then, the national obligation rests on moral considerations. It is a positional duty whose normative force derives from the moral principle that promises ought to be kept. This conclusion undermines postulate (2), which denies that the national obligation rests on moral considerations, but it casts no doubt on postulate (1), which grounds the national obligation in the relation of trusteeship between government and citizens. We have, rather, arrived at a more precise idea of what political trusteeship is and how it comes into existence.

4 Promises in moral thinking

The previous section took for granted that there are moral reasons to keep a promise. This is no sensational assumption, but it still calls for elaboration. A promise is a special obligation – a bond between particular people – as opposed to an impersonal duty deriving from consequentialist or deontological principles. To clarify the contrast, it may be useful to ask what role promises would play in moral thinking if it were based exclusively on impersonal or impartial considerations. If, for example, we were approaching moral problems from a purely consequentialist point of view, a promise would be binding only if its fulfillment was required on general, consequentialist grounds. This is to say that the promise as such would have no normative force. There would be no reason to discharge it unless the promised action was required because of its consequences. For utilitarians, in particular, the action must contribute more than any available alternative to general welfare or happiness. Nothing could be said for it if it is inferior on this score. William Godwin hints at such a reductionist view of promissory obligation. He contends that "[t]he adherence to promises ... must be ... maintained only so far as, upon a comprehensive view, it shall be found productive of a balance of happiness" (Godwin [1798] 1976, p. 227). On this view, the fact that a commitment has been made counts for nothing in its own right. The promisor must have decisive *independent* reasons to perform it.

Commitments may, to be sure, have causal effects that come into the picture when people estimate the probable consequences of keeping or breaking their words. Thus, it makes me more worse off if I do not get a treat I have been promised than if I simply have to do without it. And if, more generally, words are rarely kept, the good effects of long-term planning will be beyond reach. Yet, a comprehensive, consequentialist assessment will under certain circumstances justify breach of trust, and if it does, the very existence of a promise is neither here nor there. It matters only by virtue of how much causal difference it makes.

As it turns out, even stout utilitarians find this view hard to retain. Godwin, for one, falls back upon the common idea that promises matter in their own right, so that their normative force cannot be reduced to impersonal and impartial reasons for performing them.

> What I have promised is what I ought to have performed, if no promise had intervened, or it is not. It is conducive, or not conducive, to the generating of human happiness. If it be the former, the promise comes in merely as an additional inducement, in favour of that which, in the eye of morality, was already of indispensable obligation. ...
>
> ...But promises will not always come in reinforcement of that which was the duty before the promise was made. When it is otherwise, there is obviously a contention between what would have been obligatory, if no promise had intervened, and what the promise which has been given has a tendency to render obligatory. (Godwin [1798] 1976, pp. 218–219)

The argument involves two assumptions. If, on the one hand, someone promises something that he has reason to do in any case, the promise adds an "additional inducement" over and above the other reasons involved. And if, on the other hand, someone pledges to do a thing that, disregarding the promise, should not be done, then his promise still tends to render the action in question obligatory. While it may be an illegitimate act, all things considered, a "contention" arises that would not exist if it were not for the promise. This argument presupposes that promises matter in their own right. It is the conventional view of promissory obligation.

Where does the normative force of promises come from if it cannot be reduced to impersonal considerations? Different explanations have been given. On one view, the promisee has a right to demand that the promisor does what he has promised. Breach of trust is first and foremost presumptuous conduct – a failure to comply with legitimate claims which shows the promisor to be disrespectful of rightful (if temporary and limited) authority. But one may also see things from the opposite point of view, focusing on the vulnerability rather than the authority of the promisee. Promises provide a basis for predicting how people will behave, and such predictions are borne out only if people keep their words. Hence, a promisee is at the mercy of the promisor. He premises his actions on expectations that the promise invites and so becomes vulnerable to deception. Thus, if I provide someone with unreliable information about my future conduct, I contribute to undermining his practical rationality. Deceiving people is like leading them astray, trapping them, getting them to guide their actions by false premises. The wrongness of breaking one's word is, accordingly, not that one fails to respect the promisee's temporary authority, but rather that one takes so lightly his vulnerability.

The last argument applies just as much to positional duties as to the commitments people exchange in the course of everyday, non-institutionalized interaction. If a lawyer lets his client down, he obstructs the client's efforts to further his interests. If a cabinet minister or a public official does not live up to the responsibilities of their positions, they let down the people who have conferred authority on them. Thus, the reason why promises bind also explains why the positional duty of government officials is binding and, accordingly, why a government should look after national interests. Here, I believe, lies the ultimate justification of the national obligation.

I distinguished in the last section of chapter 1 between three roles that a moral consideration can play in practical reasoning. First, it can create a *prima facie* reason of action: a reason of immediate but uncertain appeal. Second, it can give rise to a *pro tanto* reason that is always relevant, but still defeasible. Third, it can engender a conclusive reason that tells us what, all things considered, ought to be done. The previous argument indicates that a promise falls in the middle category. As long as it is voluntary and informed, it should always be accorded some weight when it comes to judgments of right and wrong. This conclusion can be carried over to the interpretation of the national obligation. As it coincides with a positional duty which is modelled on a promise, political leaders have a *pro tanto* reason to fulfill this obligation by discharging their positional duty.

One may object that there is virtually no limit to the contents of promises in general and positional obligations in particular, and the previous paragraph seemingly entails that a "member of the SS, because he is a member of the SS, may have had a duty to exterminate various people", this being one of the things he has pledged himself to do (Stocker 1970, p. 602). How can we avoid this repugnant implication of the view that promises are *pro tanto* reasons of action? One way around it is to say that there are limits to what people may legitimately bind themselves to do; another is to avow that every promise has some normative force, which, however, is dwarfed by countervailing considerations in cases like that of the SS officer.[11] The latter view accords best with the argument of the previous section, and I believe its repugnant implications take on a bearable look when they prove immaterial from a practical point of view.

What, then, about the third assumption of Kennan's argument, which says that the national obligation is not just a *pro tanto* consideration, but a consideration with absolute priority in foreign policy? So far, this postulate has not been paid explicit attention, and it is neither disproved nor confirmed by the argument above. On the one hand, the idea that the national obligation is a positional duty modeled on a promise does not rule out that it has absolute priority and outweighs all other considerations in terms of normative force. On the other hand, I have said nothing so far to support such a strong conclusion. One may appreciate the normative force of promises without putting in a general claim to the effect that they always outweigh other considerations. Indeed, this claim sounds quite implausible. The farthest one may reasonably go is to ask if *certain* momentous promises constitute conclusive moral considerations. Does, in particular, the national obligation rest on a promise that generates a conclusive reason of action, not just a *pro tanto* reason of the kind that comes with every promise? I shall put off this question until the next chapter. The present one closes with a discussion of which specific interests the national obligation directs political leaders to pursue.

5 Defining national interests

General claims about the duty to promote national interests say nothing about specific objectives of foreign policy. We need to ask which particular interests fall under the national obligation. Kennan's argument suggests an answer, singling out three objectives as particularly important: the provision of military security, the protection of political integrity and the promotion of economic prosperity. This is a far cry from specifying political goals in operational terms, but it gives a clear indication of how political leaders should define their priorities. We shall see if the argument points in the right direction.

The notion of interest is equivocal, as there are two ways of determining what interests a person has. One may, on the one hand, ask what goods he desires or which states of affairs he wants to see in effect. Or one may, on the other hand, find out what it would be good for him to have or experience, regardless of whether he actually wants it. These approaches reflect different conceptions of what an interest is. In the first, *subjectivist* view, a person's preferences determine what interests he has, while the second, *objectivist* conception presupposes criteria of good and bad that are independent of how people appreciate things and evaluate states of affairs. Such criteria underlie assertions like S.I. Benn's: "It might be in [a] child's interest to deny him satisfaction of his desires to save him from becoming the sort of person who habitually desires the wrong sort of thing" (quoted in Swanton 1980, p. 84).[12]

If national interests are construed in subjectivist terms, the national obligation implies that foreign policy should reflect the preferences of the people. This may imply, at the extreme, that a government has no right to question, modify or set aside a cause that citizens endorse. If, by contrast, national interests are defined in objectivist terms, they are goals that should be pursued because they serve the nation well, regardless of whether citizens appreciate this or not. Foreign policy must then be guided by assumptions about a nation's true ends: what is objectively good for its citizens. The latter perspective underlies Kennan's association of the national obligation with three specific national interests: security, integrity and prosperity. These are singled out without reference to public preferences. Kennan asserts that security, integrity and prosperity are a nation's true needs.

What can be said for this idea? Its objectivist flavour runs against democratic values. Consulting the historical record, we see that democracy brings a predominantly subjectivist outlook in its train. It is a political system built around the notion that public policy should be shaped by the preferences of citizens. Thus, democracy is basically incongruous with the notion of interests whose importance can be ascertained without finding out what people actually want. Democratic leaders rarely deflate the authority of popular opinion.[13] One may ask, however, if democracy is bound up with respect for popular preferences only in domestic matters, not with regard to foreign policy.[14] An important defence of democratic institutions, which may be called the liberal argument, gives no reason for differentiating between internal and external politics in this way. Its basic premise is that everyone should be free to lead their lives according to their own goals and beliefs, provided only that they allow other people the same opportunity and otherwise treat them with due respect (e.g., by observing deontological and consequentialist constraints). They should therefore be allowed extensive influence over political decisions that shape social institutions which in turn constrain and channel individual actions and thus affect the extent to which people can live according to their personal goals and beliefs. No person is free if such decisions are taken over his head, and as democracy is the only political system that provides all citizens with extensive rights of participation, it is, *ipso facto*, the only system that may safeguard individual freedom. (This is not to say, of course, that democracy guarantees freedom; the mere mention of majority tyranny will dispel that illusion, but if proper constitutional provisions are taken, democratic institutions grant people a more extensive control over their lives than can be had under any other political system.) The liberal argument implies that citizens are not only justified in taking control over domestic legislation; their opinion is also entitled to be heard and honoured in the handling of foreign affairs. The more laws and policies of all kinds reflect popular goals and beliefs, the better, other things being equal. This is to say that the liberal argument goes hand in hand with a subjectivist interpretation of national interests. It undercuts the postulate of *raison d'état* that portrays security, integrity and prosperity as the true needs and objective interests of a nation.

On closer scrutiny, however, liberal and democratic values turn out to be compatible with some versions of the view that there are objective national interests. Sometimes public opinion forms prematurely, before enough is known to arrive at considered estimates of how different policies will affect the nation. This results in rash judgments about national priorities which may subsequently be reconsidered and revised. Whence should the government then take its guidance? Should it respect popular preferences regardless of quality, or rather model itself on the Burkean ideal of a representative who not only places the interests of constituents above his own, but "also owes them his own judgement of what is best" (Barry 1965, p. 226)? Democratic principles are basically at odds with the Burkean ideal. They imply that no government should set aside popular preferences without a good explanation. Sometimes, to be sure, preferences are legitimately overruled, as when people do not live up to minimum requirements of sanity,[15] but democratic practices presuppose that such radical mental shortcoming is rare. People are normally capable of dealing competently with practical problems. Yet, if they are carried away by strong emotions, a tension arises between democratic principles and prudential considerations.

George Kennan, for one, acknowledges this tension. He is, on the one hand, a democrat, holding that the "popular will ... expressed through the regular process of government is the only motivating impulse the government is capable of knowing and recognizing" (Kennan in a letter of January 2 1955; quoted in Hare and Joynt 1982, p. 43). In the long run, moreover, the people – or, rather, their elected representatives – can be trusted to deal competently with international matters. On the other hand, people sometimes display bad judgment. "I would like to emphasize", Kennan (1951, p. 93) says, "that I do not consider public reaction to foreign-policy questions to be erratic and undependable over the long term; but I think the record indicates that in the short term our public opinion ... can be easily led astray into areas of emotionalism and subjectivity which make it a poor and inadequate guide for national action." In view of this, he proposes a "more effective use of the principle of professionalism in the conduct of foreign policy", which is to say that decisions should be trusted to people of "insight and experience".[16] Yet, the tension between considerations of rationality and democratic principles remains. A "corps of professional officers" does not fit easily in with other elements of a political system wedded to democratic control; it runs "counter to strong prejudices and preconceptions in sections of our public mind" (ibid., p. 94).

It is arguable that democratic principles should be hedged in by considerations of rationality. In chapter 3, I shall stress that political leaders must not let personal emotions interfere with their handling of foreign affairs, and one may ask if they must likewise resist the influence of emotional impulses coming from the people. There is a crucial difference between the two cases. Even if a political leader is wrong to let national citizens suffer the consequences of *his* folly, he should not necessarily protect them against their own emotional agitation. As long as they fulfill basic requirements of sanity, it seems unjustified to interfere with their choices on paternalistic grounds. If so, popular emotionalism will not normally give ground to overrule popular preferences and thus depart from the subjectivist conception of national interests.

But there is a second, stronger reason why democratic leaders should sometimes follow their own sensible judgment rather than popular preferences. The role of the people will be limited by the fact that they sometimes react too slowly, rather than rashly and emotionally, to international events and developments. These events commonly pose unexpected problems and create situations of pressing choice, and it would be irrational, if not impracticable, to tie down foreign policy by detailed political programmes that have been cleared in advance with national citizens. This was realized already by John Locke, who accords greater prerogatives to the government in external affairs ("federative power") than in domestic matters ("executive power"):

> [T]hough this federative power in the well and ill management of it be of great moment to the commonwealth, yet it is much less capable to be directed by antecedent, standing, positive laws than the executive, and so must necessarily be left to the prudence and wisdom of those hands it is in, to be managed for the public good. For the laws that concern subjects one amongst another, being to direct their actions, may well enough precede them. But what is to be done in reference to foreigners depending much upon their actions, and the variation of designs and interests, must be left in great part to the prudence of those who have this power committed to them, to be managed by the best of their skill for the advantage of the commonwealth. (Locke [1690] 1984, sect. 146, pp. 191–192)

Locke's point is that a government cannot await the formation of public opinion before it handles pressing issues that are imposed on it by other countries. The urge to keep up with quickly shifting international challenges is not easily reconciled with respect for an often slow democratic process. A government that pays too much attention to popular opinion will not be flexible enough in its handling of foreign affairs. If a pressing situation arises and political leaders cannot await the people's verdict, they must either take their guidance from priorities that previously have been voiced through the democratic process, or, if no clear precedence exists, fall back on their own considered judgments. In the latter case, political decisions will have to be based on what a government believes *really* benefits national citizens. This argument, which shows that national interests cannot always be inferred from popular preferences, opens the door to an objectivist conception of such interests. Yet, the negative claim that subjectively defined interests should not guide democratic leaders under all circumstances is far weaker than a postulate to the effect that some goals – security, integrity and prosperity – are objective interests of all states.

To come closer to Kennan's postulate, consider a third objection to the view that national interests must always be defined in subjectivist terms. This says that national interests will rarely be definable at all if they are to be defined subjectively. Citizens often disagree about political priorities, and when they do, it makes no sense to talk about "what they want" as if they all wanted the same thing. If preferences diverge, we cannot speak of public opinion in the singular and have no basis for defining national interests in subjective terms. This argument is quite general. It poses a challenge to all statements about collective goals and common interests, whether they turn on domestic matters or foreign affairs. The basic premise that preferences often conflict is voiced most insistently in Marxist literature, which stresses class antagonism as the crux of political life. But it is a chord often struck even by liberal analysts, who assume that pulling and hauling among interest-groups pervade political life. Stephen Krasner (1978, p. 26) points out that "liberalism, like Marxism, begins with the society", and that both perspectives depict politics "as a competition among organized interests. ... In its most simplified and schematic form, interest-group theories view politics as a vector diagram in which a series of pressures are brought to bear on the state, which then moves in the direction it is pushed by the strongest societal forces."

One way of getting around the problem is to question its premises on empirical grounds. Conflicting preferences may not characterize political life as much as some analysts think. Many objectives of foreign policy are in fact subject to widespread agreement. Joseph Frankel (1970, p. 43) claims, for example, that agreement occurs much more frequently in this area than in domestic politics:

> [I]n domestic politics ... the divergence of competing interests is striking and ... it is possible to deny the very existence of anything called 'general' or 'public' interest. In foreign policy, it is impossible to deny altogether the existence of a national interest, however vague and nebulous it may appear to be, at least as an important datum. Here, in the absence of similar divergences and clashes between sectional interests, a basic agreement on national interest as a whole is much more readily reached.

I shall, however, set greater store by another response to the problem of conflicting preferences. It says that social antagonism may loom large without undercutting every possibility of convergent popular preferences. Two examples should serve to bring out this point. First, practically all citizens will have a common interest in fending off external challenges that threaten to thwart any domestically supported policy, however much they remain at loggerheads over the use of the resulting opportunities. This implies, more specifically, that the problem of conflicting preferences has limited relevance with respect to certain aspects of security policy. Whatever view a person takes of domestic matters, he has an interest in preserving national independence. Secondly, all citizens have an interest in increasing aggregate national wealth, despite the existence of domestic distributive conflict. The more resources a state has, the more citizens can spend on their favourite projects, whichever they favour. These examples bring out the idea that "a policy, law or institution is in someone's interest if it increases his opportunities to get what he wants – whatever that may be" (Barry 1967, p. 115). Such opportunities make the pursuit of any national goal easier than it would otherwise have been. The more they obtain, the better people can implement democratic decisions reflecting their preferences. But when we are to identify the opportunities in question, there is no need to chart popular objectives by asking what people actually want. We must rather find out how their prospect of pursuing any objective at all can be improved. It is in everyone's interest that this prospect is as good as possible, and it must be defined in objective terms, with reference to real obstacles and opportunities of effective political action.

The last argument supports Kennan's objectivist interpretation of national interests. It is arguable that security, integrity and prosperity are among the objective conditions of any successful national policy. Hence, a government can effectuate democratic decisions only if it also sees to it that these conditions prevail. It is even arguable that security, integrity and prosperity are the most important national interests, regardless of what other interests citizens embrace through the democratic process. The point is that most national objectives will come to naught if military security is neglected, national integrity withers or the economy falters. It is a question of basic opportunities of effective political action.

But what if many citizens want a policy that deliberately or predictably undermines one or more of these opportunities? What, for example, if they want their state to abandon integrity by subordinating itself to another state, or if they go in for national disarmament that erodes security? What should political leaders then do? Does it follow from democratic principles that a government must abide by popular preferences even if this means destroying basic opportunities of effective political action? It obviously depends on how strong the preferences in question are. Are they voiced by a minority, a majority or the whole population? According to an enshrined principle of most democracies, qualified majorities are required for the legitimate adoption of policies that radically or irreversibly changes the *status quo*. This is to say that a large majority of citizens must stand behind a policy undermining security, integrity and prosperity before a government should set out to implement it. If, say, nine-tenths of the population go in for national disarmament, political leaders can hardly refuse to disarm by citing the objective need of national defence. If their principal – national citizens – care little about this need, it cannot be decisive of how political leaders ought to discharge their obligation as trustees. But if disarmament is advocated only by a bare majority, things stand differently. Then political leaders may be justified in preserving security, which is a basic opportunity of effective political action, rather than acting on preferences that many citizens reject and whose implementation would undermine the opportunity in question. Although this policy has no indisputable justification, it does not obviously violate democratic principles. This explains the special status of national interests pertaining to security, integrity and prosperity. These interests can be attributed to states without reference to popular preferences, and they should be pursued by any government unless citizens have strong preferences to the contrary.

There is no obvious and indisputable way of drawing the line between public preferences that are too weak to weigh with a government when basic opportunities are at stake, and preferences that are strong enough. Just how widely must national citizens support, say, disarmament before it should become official policy? No definite answer suggests itself. Moreover, it may sometimes be hard to determine whether a given policy does jeopardize basic opportunities of effective political action. One aspect of this problem is that goals like security and integrity permit different, even contradictory specifications. Take, for instance, the Norwegian choice between neutrality and membership in NATO. Some people held that Norway became more exposed to Soviet aggression by joining NATO in 1950, while others thought membership in the defence alliance would have the opposite effect. What the first group of citizens considered a threat to national security, the second group saw as central to Norwegian defence. There is also another aspect to the same general problem. Whether basic opportunities of political action exist or not is a matter of degree, and it is sometimes conceivable that small sacrifices in one respect may buy considerable gains in another. Thus, it is arguable that national integrity was slightly reduced when Norway, by joining NATO, renounced some sovereignty in matters of defence, but it is also arguable that the (alleged) higher level of security made for a net gain with respect to basic opportunities. In such a case, a government must base its decision on an overall estimate of negative and positive consequences, and estimates of this type are necessarily conjectural.

I shall not go further into these problems. They are best treated with reference to concrete political issues. Moreover, they do not challenge the general thrust of the argument above. A government should normally take care to preserve security, integrity and prosperity because it thereby assures that national citizens can achieve what they want, whatever that may be. The pursuit of these goals is the most important task of political leaders, and only in exceptional circumstances should foreign policy no longer be geared to this task.

6 Conclusion

The major conclusion of this chapter is that the national obligation rests on moral considerations. This shows that an interest-based foreign policy is not necessarily in opposition to a policy informed by morality. The national obligation, which says that political authorities ought to do what is best for national citizens, is a positional obligation modelled on a promise. It implies that authorities have a *pro tanto* duty of pursuing policies that are to the advantage of the nation. Moreover, this obligation calls for a special concern about primary national interests: security, integrity and prosperity. Their promotion increases the opportunity of citizens to achieve what they want, whatever that may be.

3 The Priority of National Interests

1. Introduction

How does the national obligation compare to other moral considerations in terms of normative force? Is it a conclusive reason of action or can competing considerations outweigh it? Postulate (3) of Kennan's argument states that the national obligation has absolute priority as far as military security, political integrity and economic prosperity are concerned (cf. chapter 2). This is a central tenet of the doctrine of *raison d'état*. It does not imply that every national interest always counts for more than anything else, but that a limited set of core interests, which may be called the primary national interests, come before all other considerations. I shall hereafter refer to postulate (3) as the *absolute priority principle*.

Many people who embrace the national obligation balk at the absolute priority principle. They acknowledge the normative force of national interests, but deny that a government is allowed and obligated to do what is best for national citizens regardless of how other people fare as a result. Their assumption is that the national obligation must in all cases be balanced against competing considerations, and should be discharged if and only if it is not outweighed by them. Such considerations may be of many kinds. Consider, for instance, the principle of *pacta sunt servanda* which says that a state should stand by its words and keep its agreements. This principle lies at the root of international law, and few governments or theorists dismiss it. Can it outweigh the national obligation? If so, a government that once entered into an agreement that it can later fulfill only by sacrificing primary interests, may still be obligated to fulfill it. There is no saying, of course, that agreements must be kept regardless of costs, but it may turn out that a conflict between the principle of *pacta sunt servanda* and the national obligation should be resolved in favour of the former. This possibility is ruled out by the absolute priority principle.

The purpose of this chapter is to probe the validity of the absolute priority principle as well as other ways of balancing the national obligation against competing moral considerations. It will be done in conjunction with a general discussion of trusteeship in interpersonal relations. Section 2 introduces the assumption that a trustee may rightfully do for the principal only what the principal may rightfully do in his own capacity. Section 3 suggests, by contrast, that political leaders must set aside at least some concerns that come into the picture when people pursue their personal interests. According to the absolute priority principle, they are simply obligated to do what is best for the nation unless citizens instruct them otherwise, but this idea will be rejected in section 4. Less extreme forms of national favouritism still have something to say for them. Thus, section 5 shows that political leaders, unlike people who act on their own behalf, are not free to take non-optimal courses of action. Moreover, section 6 concludes that a government should not engage in supererogation. Finally, sections 7 and 8 argue that in situations of moral indeterminacy and risk, when political leaders cannot tell for sure what is right and what is wrong, they should do what is best for the nation.

2 The thesis of equivalence

Let me begin with a general distinction between two types of action. An action is *vicarious* if it is done by one person on another person's behalf. When a mother signs a contract on behalf of her son who has not yet attained his majority, she acts vicariously, and the same goes for a government that pursues the interests of national citizens (with the trivial difference that the members of a government are also citizens). A *first-person* action, by contrast, is something someone does solely on his own behalf.

Are the things people can legitimately do on their own behalf any different from the things other persons can do for them? If not – if, in other words, the principles that regulate vicarious action coincide entirely with the principles of first-person morality – then one person will be permitted to do something on behalf of another if and only if the other is allowed to do the same thing himself. The existence of an intermediary agent makes no moral difference. Such an assumption has important implications for moral thinking about trusteeship, as a trustee acts on behalf of a principal whose interests he has pledged himself to look after. The assumption implies that the trustee may rightfully do for the principal only what the principal may rightfully do in his own capacity. This will be called the *thesis of equivalence*.

Two things follow if the thesis of equivalence is true. First, the absolute priority principle is false. A government cannot legitimately pursue national interests without regard to other states and peoples because no person can do anything he likes in the pursuit of personal interests. Everyone must, in particular, observe the harm principle, as set out in chapter 1. Thus, the national obligation is no conclusive consideration of political morality if the thesis of equivalence is true. This thesis implies, secondly, that moral assessment of vicarious action can proceed on the same premises that underlie first-person morality. The principles people are to observe when they act on their own behalf must also be observed when they act on behalf of others. If, in particular, I ought to abstain from a certain action, then a trustee will not be allowed to perform this action for me.

Yet, the thesis of equivalence does not debar a trustee from according greater importance to the fulfillment of his principal's interests than the importance their fulfillment has from an impersonal point of view. The thesis does not imply, in particular, that no measure of national partiality is permissible in the conduct of foreign policy. A government is morally permitted to favour national citizens in so far as they would be permitted to favour themselves if they were acting on their own behalf. In general, a trustee is permitted to deviate from impartiality whenever such deviation is open to the principal – in the same ways and to the same extent. If, conversely, first-person morality is bound up with an impartial outlook, the principles of vicarious action must be impartial, too. Applying this argument to the problems of foreign policy, we arrive at a position akin to that of Charles Beitz:

> In domestic affairs, few would disagree that what people have a right to have done for them is limited by what they have a right to do for themselves. For example, if people have no right to enslave ten percent of their number, their leaders have no right to do so for them. Why should the international actions of national leaders be any different? It seems that what leaders may rightfully do for their people, internationally or domestically, is limited by what the people may rightfully do for themselves. (Beitz 1979, p. 24)

Beitz's position is ambiguous on one score. He says that political leaders must keep within whatever limits citizens have to observe, but he does not say whether or not leaders are free to do everything citizens may do within these limits. The latter follows, however, from the thesis of equivalence. It says that the morality of vicarious action is in *every* respect equivalent to first-person morality.

3 Three theses of non-equivalence

The thesis of equivalence is open to challenge. One may argue that political leaders, who are responsible for many people's welfare, must set aside at least some concerns that enter into the picture when people pursue their personal interests. Thomas Nagel advances an argument to this effect:

> Public officials accept special obligations to serve interests that their offices are designed to advance ... In doing so, they correlatively reduce their right to consider other factors, both their personal interests and more general ones not related to the institution or their role in it. (Nagel 1978, p. 89)

Nagel posits the idea of a *reduced right* to consider other factors than the national interest. The reduction is depicted as a correlate of the special relationship between political authorities and national citizens. It is as if this relationship invalidates some considerations that normally weigh with people when they scrutinize their choices. According to Nagel, certain factors have no place in the deliberations of a government. Not only *can* it disregard them, it *should* do so. To lack the right to consider certain factors is to be bound to set them aside. Nagel says little, however, about what factors he has in mind. He alludes to "personal" and "general" interests, which may encompass many things, and we shall soon see that his position is open to divergent interpretations. But one thing is clear: Nagel speaks of a reduced, not a non-existent, right of public officials to consider other factors than their special obligations. The implicit assumption is that some such factors can and should be taken into account. The moral horizon is to be limited, but it cannot be confined to national interests. This assumption is confirmed by Nagel's further argument:

> Public figures ... are [not] obliged to consider only the national or state interest in arriving at their decisions as it would be a breach of responsibility to consider anything else. ... [A]ny view as absolute as this is mistaken: there are no such extreme obligations, or offices to which they attach. ... Obligations to the state also have limits, which derive from their moral context. (Nagel 1978, pp. 80–81)

This implies, in particular, that "states can remain neutral in external disputes, and can legitimately favor their own populations – though not at any cost whatever to the rest of the world" (ibid., p. 84). With this remark, Nagel distances himself from what I have called the absolute priority principle. He says, in effect, that there are limits to what a government can do to further national interests. He is not, however, very specific about the nature of these limits. They are said to derive from the "moral context" of "obligations to the state", which must be the context of other moral considerations that bear on how a government ought to act. We may call them, for short, limiting considerations. The crucial task is to specify these. They are a subset of the factors that normally enter into moral deliberation – the subset that remains after certain "personal" and "general" interests have been subtracted. Thus, limiting considerations begin where the reduction of a government's right to consider other factors end.

Nagel speaks about the relationship between government and citizens, but what he says may be recast as a general argument about trusteeship. According to this argument, any agent, by taking on the obligation of a trustee, reduces his right to consider other factors than the interests of the principal. Whether or not Nagel actually countenances this generalized rendering of his position, it is a convenient point to start examining his more specific argument about political trusteeship.

Nagel's view is compatible with many substantive views of how the obligation of trusteeship narrows down legitimate reasons of action. The number and nature of limiting considerations are an open question. A simple, stylized example will bring out one notable possibility. Assume that a trustee, T, acting on his principal P's behalf, must make a choice between three mutually exclusive actions, X, Y, and Z. The following conditions obtain: (i) The three actions can be ranked according to how they affect the interests of the principal: X is better than Y, which is better than Z. (ii) If P was acting on his own behalf, he would, according to appropriate principles of first-person morality, have a duty not to perform X, but be free to choose between Y and Z. The question is what T, who actually is to make the choice, ought to do. If the thesis of equivalence is correct, T's situation is exactly as P's would have been. He should not do X and is free to choose between Y and Z. In Nagel's view, however, things can stand differently.

In the first place, T may be obligated to choose Y – the alternative which is optimal for P among those that are permitted to him. On this view, T must do nothing but what is best for the principal, although the principal would be free to take other, non-optimal courses of action. P is, in particular, free to forego personal advantages, but T should not forego anything on P's behalf that P can justifiably have. Apart from this, there is no difference between the trustee and his principal. The former cannot set aside limiting considerations which the latter must take into account. Thus, the alternative X, which P has a duty not to perform, is morally debarred even for T. This possibility corresponds to what I shall call the *weak thesis of non-equivalence*. It does not exempt the trustee from honouring duties that weigh with the principal. His reduced right to consider other factors pertains only to his choice between actions which fall within the constraints of first-person morality. As far as these are concerned, he is obligated to do what caters best to the interests of the principal. A trustee must not, in particular, pursue personal advantages, nor should he behave whimsically, emotionally or imprudently. He is, briefly put, obligated to act optimally.

One proviso must be added to the weak thesis of non-equivalence. A trustee can – and should – act less than optimally if the principal instructs him to do so. A person who is free to sacrifice advantages on his own behalf, is also free to authorize a trustee to make such sacrifices for him. This is in line with what I said about national interests in chapter 2, with the exception only that a government should not sacrifice primary national interests – security, integrity and prosperity – unless a large majority of citizens say so. To sum up, the weak thesis of non-equivalence tells a trustee to observe the same moral constraints that weigh upon the principal and, within these constraints, to do what is best for the principal unless the principal instructs him otherwise.

This is, however, not the only possible elaboration of Nagel's argument. It also, in the second place, allows of an interpretation that divests the rules of vicarious action further from the morality of first-person behaviour. Apart from being obligated to do what is best for the principal, a trustee may be exempted from some moral concerns that the principal would have to consider if he were acting on his own behalf. The first clause runs parallel to the weak thesis of non-equivalence, while the second is an important addition. It implies that there are fewer limiting considerations on what a trustee may do for his principal than there are constraints on the things people can do for themselves.

This rendering of Nagel's argument is suggested by his assertion that public officials have a reduced right to consider "both their personal interests and more general ones not related to the institution or their role in it". In ruling out personal interests, Nagel alludes to the idea that a trustee must do what is best for his principal, but by speaking of general interests as well, he indicates that some moral constraints on first-person behaviour are not among the limiting considerations of vicarious action. Nagel says little to suggest *which* constraints, only that no government can legitimately favour its own citizens "at any cost whatever to the rest of the world". This points to the obvious relevance of how costly an action is to other people when it comes to determining whether or not a principal is free to perform this action. If we contemplate the possibility that some first-person considerations have no bearing on vicarious action, the less urgent ones must be the first to go. They are thought to be urgent enough to weigh with people when they act on their own behalf, but are outweighed by the obligation of trusteeship. I shall call this the *moderate thesis of non-equivalence*. It may be summed up by saying that a trustee should do what is best for the principal, unless the principal instructs him otherwise, within the limits of the most urgent considerations pertaining to how his actions affect other people.

There is a third way in which the situation of a trustee can differ from that of a principal. It is ruled out by Nagel's argument, but was suggested by the absolute priority principle. It divests the morality of vicarious action altogether from the rules of first-person behaviour. On this view, a trustee is quite simply obligated to do what is best for the principal unless the principal instructs him otherwise. No other consideration must be taken into account. This will be called the *strong thesis of non-equivalence*. It entails the absolute priority principle. The idea that a government should place primary national interests before all other considerations in the conduct of foreign policy is a special version of the claim that a trustee must always do what is best for the principal.

The rest of the chapter will discuss the thesis of equivalence and the three theses of non-equivalence. Let me first, however, look at how these conflicting assumptions about the relationship between first-person morality and the rules of vicarious action square with the general account of trusteeship given in chapter 2. I argued that the obligation of a trustee is basically at one with the obligation deriving from a promise. Following William Godwin, a distinction was drawn between two ways in which a promise may influence moral deliberation. If what I have promised to do is what I ought to do in any case, the promise is just an "additional inducement" to do the right thing. But if the promised action is in itself wrong (because of its consequences or inherent characteristics), then there is, as Godwin says, a "contention" between what I ought to have done if no promise had been made, and "what the promise which has been given has a tendency to render obligatory". The strong thesis of non-equivalence falls squarely on Godwin's account of promises. If a trustee should always honour his promissory commitments, there can be no contention between what he ought to have done if he had made no promise and what the promise tends to render obligatory. His promise settles the case conclusively. However, the other assumptions invoked above run parallel to Godwin's account. The weak and the moderate thesis of non-equivalence, as well as the thesis of equivalence, imply that the promise of a trustee may override some, but not all other considerations of first-person morality. This is to say that there exists a contention in Godwin's sense between these constraints and the special obligation of political leaders towards national citizens. According to the weak and the strong thesis of non-equivalence, this contention is stronger with respect to the special obligation of trusteeship than in the case of ordinary promises. The thesis of equivalence, by contrast, implies that the contention arises to the same extent for all kinds of promissory obligation.

4 The rejection of absolute priority

The absolute priority principle is central to the doctrine of *raison d'état*. It implies that a government can take every necessary step to defend national security, integrity and prosperity. It need not, as Kennan says, accept any moral reproach for promoting primary national interests. On the face of it, the absolute priority principle is implausible. An individual citizen or a group of citizens who act on their own behalf are not free to pursue their interests without regard to other people. They should, in particular, take the harm principle into consideration, and it seems strange that a government can rightfully disregard something which weighs so heavily with people in general. It will, indeed, be free to do so only if the morality of vicarious action diverges radically from the rules of first-person behaviour. Does it? The following hypothetical example suggests an answer:

> *Case I.* T, who is entrusted the management of P's firm, is aware that a competing firm poses a serious challenge to P's business interests. The competing firm is lead by a shrewd entrepreneur who cannot be defeated by commercial means. Realizing this, T sees to it that the leader of the competing firm suffers a fatal accident by tampering with the brakes of his car.

In view of the pledge T has made, is he right to do what he does? In itself, the action is surely wrong, and it would clearly have been impermissible for P himself to sabotage the car of the shrewd entrepreneur. He faces fierce competition, but this does not permit him to do just anything in defence of his interests. By sabotaging the car, he would perpetrate harm that is both grave in itself and out of proportion to the damage he would otherwise suffer. If P cannot fend off competition by other means, he will have to bite the dust. Now, does the fact that another person performs the dubious action on P's behalf alter its moral status? According to the strong thesis of non-equivalence, it does, but this just shows that the thesis must be wrong. To suggest that T's obligation to P in Case I overrides all other considerations is a travesty of common moral sense. No assumption with such contra-intuitive implications can stand.

It may be objected that the relationship between a government and its citizens is a special type of trusteeship, and that a conclusion about interpersonal relations does not carry over to political life. If so, the strong thesis of non-equivalence may be valid with respect to foreign policy even if it is invalid in Case I. This objection does not hold, however. An international analogue of Case I would be a government that defends its nation's share of international trade by blowing up other states' production facilities or sinking ships that carry their exports. Such measures are clearly immoral.

In response to this argument, a more restricted version of the strong thesis of non-equivalence may be suggested. As indicated above, the harm T perpetrates in defence of P's interests is out of proportion to the harm P will suffer if his firm loses markets. Case I is an *asymmetric* conflict of interest: P risks only economic loss, while the owner of the competing firm is attacked by potentially fatal means.[17] Consider, by way of contrast, another hypothetical case:

> *Case II.* T is entrusted the protection of P's life. He sees a man stepping out from a crowd with a gun pointed at P. The only way T can be sure to save P's life is by shooting the man with the gun. If he shoots, however, he risks hitting other people in the crowd. T fires two shots; the first misses its target and fatally wounds a bystander; the second shot is a hit.

In Case II, a *symmetric* conflict of interest exists between P and the man with the gun. It is, moreover, a symmetric conflict involving the most urgent kinds of human interest. Life is pitted against life. The man threatens P's life, and the threat can only be deflected by means of force. Is it permissible to deflect it in this potentially fatal way? If the man with the gun had not been surrounded by a crowd, the case would, in most people's view, have been open and shut. It is widely believed that a person has a right to defend his life against deadly threats by means of force, and that a trustee has no less of a right to defend the life of his principal by such means. To be sure, this belief is disputed by pacifists, whose view of the matter will be discussed in chapter 4, but can be set aside for the moment. The important point at present is that even those – or many of those – who hold that people can legitimately be defended against violence by means of force, stop to ask whether it is really right that the trustee fires at the would-be murderer in Case II.

The problem is, of course, that there are other people in the picture besides P and the man with the gun. They can aptly be characterized as *innocent bystanders*. What T does to defend P's life fatally wounds one of these – a person who in no way threatens P. We may suppose, moreover, that T has every reason to believe that a shot aimed at the man with the gun risks hitting an innocent bystander instead. This is to say that there is a symmetric conflict of interest between P and the innocent bystanders. P's life can only be defended by threatening their lives. The only way this conflict differs from that between P and the man with the gun, is that the latter conflict is provoked by a person with murderous designs while the former is accidental in the sense that neither party has such designs on the other.

It seems clear to me that the presence of innocent bystanders implies that Case II is not, after all, open and shut. To think otherwise, one must either (1) reject the harm principle altogether, which is out of the question, or (2) argue that a trustee may (and must) sometimes – notably in symmetric conflicts of interest where life is at stake – care only about the interests of his principal. (2) is tantamount to invoking a restricted version of the strong thesis of non-equivalence. It implies that, owing to the special characteristics of Case II, T can altogether disregard the fate of everyone save P. This idea is absurd, and its absurdity shows that the strong thesis of non-equivalence is wrong even in restricted form. The killing of a bystander is, in itself, no less tragic than the killing of P would have been. The need to defend one innocent person cannot render the life of another less significant.

This is not to say, of course, that the trustee is necessarily wrong in doing what he does in Case II. He might, all things considered, be right to defend his principal's life at the risk of killing innocent bystanders. Nothing I have said so far rules out that the harm principle is overridden by P's right of self-defence, vicariously executed by T. The point is only that questions have to be asked, no less about T's vicarious action than about P's reaction if his defence were in his own hands. To set aside the harm principle without further ado is quite different from balancing it against competing considerations and concluding that the latter weigh it up.

As a last-ditch attempt to rescue the strong thesis of non-equivalence, one might suggest that its restricted version is valid at least with respect to *political* action. The assumption would be that a government that defends the most urgent interests of national citizens can disregard all other moral constraints, although trustees cannot generally do so. Is there something to this view? Consider an international analogue of Case II. The government of state A has reliable information that a missile has been sent toward its territory by a hostile state, B. The course of the missile is set for a populated area in A. The only way of stopping it is to shoot it down, which has to be done while it passes over the territory of a neighbouring country, C. A's defensive missile system can do the job, but it is highly likely that a collision of missiles in the air will cause an explosion that kills many people on the ground. These will be inhabitants of C – innocent bystanders, whose lives are protected by the harm principle. What should the government of A do? I can see no reason for it to approach this problem differently from how T ought to approach his problem in Case II. The government must balance the harm principle, which tells against shooting down the missile, against considerations of defence. It cannot escape the question whether or not citizens of A are right, all things considered, to protect themselves in the suggested way. No answer need be given here, but the need to answer before acting is obvious. (In chapter 5 I shall look closer at situations in which national interests can be pursued only by means that harm innocent people.)

The previous argument, although inconclusive in some important respects, is a conclusive refutation of the absolute priority principle. It proves, accordingly, that a central tenet of the doctrine of *raison d'état* has to go. A government cannot favour national interests to the extent of totally disregarding other moral considerations.

5 Non-equivalence and rationality

I argued in section 4 that there is no difference between vicarious action and first-person behaviour as far as the importance of the harm principle in concerned. A *pro tanto* duty not to harm innocent people rests with those who act on their own behalf as well as those who act on behalf of others. The introduction of an intermediary agent makes no moral difference on this score. This is not to say, however, that vicarious action should in every respect follow the rules of first-person behaviour. To reject the strong thesis of non-equivalence is not tantamount to embracing the thesis of equivalence. I have, indeed, suggested two intermediary positions – the *weak* and the *moderate* thesis of non-equivalence (cf. section 3). They divest the rules of vicarious action from first-person morality, but only to a limited extent. Both positions are compatible with what was said in the previous section, as neither implies that a trustee can disregard everything save the interests of the principal.

I shall first confront the thesis of equivalence and the weak thesis of non-equivalence. The latter says, to recall, that a trustee should observe the same moral constraints that weigh upon the principal and, within these constraints, do what is best for the principal unless the principal instructs him otherwise. This drives a wedge between first-person behaviour and vicarious action. Thus, a person who acts on his own behalf is always free to choose non-optimal actions, but such freedom is incompatible with the obligation of trusteeship.

The weak thesis of non-equivalence accords with plausible – indeed trivial – assumptions about trusteeship in inter-personal relations. First, a person who has taken on responsibility for another is not allowed to exploit this position for his private purposes. He may, of course, get paid for the job or otherwise find it rewarding, but beyond this it must not be a vehicle for his enrichment or reward. Acting as a trustee, he should not let personal reasons interfere with what he does. Second, a trustee should aspire to rationality in his fulfillment of the role's requirements. This idea has no counterpart in first-person morality. If a grown-up person wastes his personal belongings, giving in to imprudent impulses or letting himself be carried away by irrational emotions, he is not morally at fault. But if this person squanders resources that he has pledged himself to administer for another, he is acting not just foolishly but wrongly. This is obvious when trusteeship is established to protect the interests of people who are incapable of looking after themselves, but it goes even for those who are engaged on other grounds to stand in for others. Any trustee would fail to honour the obligations of his role if frivolous reasons were allowed to influence his performance of it.

Is the relationship between government and citizens any different from ordinary trusteeship on these scores? Consider, first, the place of personal reasons in political deliberation. In the sixteenth century, when political theorists began arguing about statecraft as a question of furthering the interests of the state, it was not always clear whose interests came into the picture. The goals of governments were often associated with the personal interests of political leaders. The crucial concern was to preserve governmental authority by warding off external and internal challenges. This outlook leaves its mark on the first major treatise on statecraft – Machiavelli's *The Prince* – which considers "how … princedoms can be governed and preserved" and how a prince should act so to "retain [-] his position" (Machiavelli [1531] 1975, ch. 2, p. 59). But this is not the sole – nor, perhaps, the dominant – purpose of Machiavelli's complete work. According to Friedrich Meinecke ([1924] 1962), parts of *The Prince* "can easily arouse the feeling that Machiavelli is only watching out for the personal advantage of the prince" (ibid., p. 41), but a different impression emerges when this book is juxtaposed to *The Discourses*. "One sees clearly", Meinecke says, "what is the real central idea in Machiavelli's life: namely, the regeneration of a fallen people by means of the *virtù* of a tyrant." Machiavelli moved "on the ethical heights of a *raison d'état* … which was capable of a vital consciousness of the good of the community, the *bene commune* of the whole people" (ibid., p. 44).

In modern political theory, there are few traces of Machiavelli's ambiguity on this score. The idea that political leaders should pursue national interests rather than their own good is firmly entrenched. It seems obvious today that they must not use political positions for enriching themselves or aspiring to personal honour. It is less obvious, but hardly controversial, that leaders should not let themselves be carried away by personal hatred or other emotional inclinations in the handling of foreign policy. Frivolous reasons have no place in their deliberations. This assumption can be traced to the very idea of interest-governed activity, which evokes a contrast between prudence and emotional agitation. The notion of 'interest' was originally coined to denote the opposite of whimsical, impulsive and passionate motives in political life. It was used by Machiavelli and others to criticize policies that give vent to "personal inclinations and aversions", which let loose the "lower elemental forces" or express "merely instinctive greed" (Meinecke [1924] 1962, pp. 6, 52, and 152).

Consider, as an illustration, Anthony Eden's performance during the Suez crisis in 1956. The British Prime Minister saw to it that his country collaborated with France and Israel in launching a military attack to stop Egypt's expropriation of the Suez Canal Company. Different considerations may be invoked to criticize this policy, but we are only interested in assessing it on grounds of rationality. Whatever view one takes of Egyptian policy, there is no denying the large element of fervent passion in Eden's motivation when he made the crucial decisions. He corresponded with Thucydides' (1972, bk. 3, pp. 243–244) description of Greek statesmen at the time of the Peloponnesian war: "always ready to satisfy the hatreds of the hour". Eden's hatred was directed at the Egyptian President Gamal Abdul Nasser. In his memoirs, written less than five years after the events, Eden speaks of Nasser as a "megalomaniacal dictator" with a "streak of paranoia", who aimed at "dominating a large part of the world" (Eden 1960, pp. 430–431). To those who "say that Nasser is no Hitler or Mussolini", Eden replies: "Allowing for a difference in scale, I am not so sure" (ibid., p. 431). But the difference in scale makes so much difference in this case that Eden's analogy is quite inapposite as a basis of rational policy. Regardless of whether Nasser was in the grips of megalomania, his meager means gave grounds to deflate his rhetoric. Eden's actions seem motivated more by personal hatred than an assessment of how Britain's national interests could best be advanced.

In general, political leaders should not let frivolous reasons enter into their deliberations. Doing so is clearly at odds with their special obligation towards citizens. Here lies a general distinction between first-person behaviour and vicarious action. An agent is free to act non-optimally when he acts on his own behalf, but if he acts on behalf of another, he must do what he can to follow an optimal course of action. The role of trustee merges morality and rationality in the sense that the latter becomes part of the former.

This implies that the thesis of equivalence is wrong. The rules of vicarious action do not derive fully from the morality of first-person behaviour. Thus, Thomas Nagel is correct to say that a trustee – and a government in particular – has a reduced right to consider other factors than the interests of the principal. The weak thesis of non-equivalence is a first indication of how far the reduction goes. It remains to see if it goes even further than this thesis suggests.

6 Non-equivalence and supererogatory action

The moderate thesis of non-equivalence goes one step further than the weak thesis in distinguishing the rules of vicarious action from the morality of first-person behaviour. It says that a trustee is obligated to do what is best for the principal unless the principal instructs him otherwise, subject only to the constraint that he observes the most urgent considerations pertaining to how his actions affect other people. This is to say that the obligation of trusteeship annuls some otherwise relevant but *less* urgent moral considerations. Does it?

In order to distinguish between moral considerations in terms of urgency, I shall start by differentiating two perspectives on morality. Most often, moral thinking is a question of finding out how people ought to act. The question of right action is, in particular, at the center of this book. It addresses moral matters from a *practical* perspective that typically concludes in assertions about rights and duties – moral categories which are meant to tell people what they may do and which constraints they have to observe. But moral thinking does not only relate to reasons of action, it also turns on questions of value. We say, for example, that a person like Mother Theresa, who devotes her life to working among the poor, does something very valuable. Her efforts deserve our greatest admiration. Such assertions represent the *valuative* perspective of moral thinking. Now, the distinction between the two perspectives may be of analytical interest only. It is arguable that every valuative assertion has practical implications. The fact that a person does something valuable implies that there are moral reasons for her to do as she does and perhaps good reasons for others to emulate her. Value assessments may, in other words, be bound up with practical recommendations. It is also conceivable, however, that the valuative and the practical perspective do not come to one. There may sometimes be reason to admire an action although the agent had no moral reason for doing what he did. As a simple illustration, imagine that a shipwreck has taken place and two persons are drifting afloat at sea. By chance, one has got hold of two lifebelts, which are the only lifebelts in sight. There are certainly moral reasons for him to pass one belt to the other person. Most people would say that he has a duty to do so. But what if he has only got hold of only one lifebelt – the only one in sight? He has, then, no duty to give this belt to the other person.[18] Doing so would certainly be praiseworthy, a noble thing, an action of tremendous moral value, but it would not be morally required, and the person in question could not be blamed for not giving away the only lifebelt. We are considering a *supererogatory* action. It has a great value, but its value does not translate into a reason of action.

The existence of supererogatory actions shows that the valuative perspective of moral thinking can diverge from the practical perspective. The worth of such actions notwithstanding, they lie beyond the call of duty. They evoke admiration, but no one is obligated to perform them. This may appear paradoxical. After all, if one act is better than another and both are feasible, do we not have a good (if not necessarily conclusive) reason to opt for the best? Some simply say no, arguing that certain expectations are unreasonable, however valuable their fulfillment might be. Those who fail to perform supererogatory actions are in no way doing things that they ought not to have done (Heyd 1982, ch. 6). Others advance a somewhat different argument, suggesting that we distinguish between two senses of the moral 'ought'. In the ordinary sense of the word, the things we ought to do are required of us, and it would be wrong not to do them unless conflicting requirements provide even stronger reasons to act otherwise. But there is also a discretionary sense of 'ought', in which we can leave the things we ought to do undone without doing anything wrong. In James Fishkin's words, "it would be admirable or virtuous if we were to do what we 'ought', but no one could reasonably blame us if we did not" (Fishkin 1982, p 11). Thus, acts of self-denial, like passing the only life belt to another person, are signs of uncommon goodness, and although everyone ought live as well as he can, the performance of these actions is still a discretionary matter.

There is no need here to determine whether the notion of a discretionary ought is well taken. The important thing is that no one attaches any requirement to discretionary actions although everyone welcomes their performance. In so far as the high value of such actions give rise to practical considerations, these are considerations that people need not take into account, although they may do so, and although their doing so is not a matter of moral indifference: it is definitely better that they do than that they do not.

What has just been said about supererogation applies to first-person behaviour. Vicarious action is, however, different. It does not normally allow for supererogation. While it is praiseworthy of a person to endure losses himself rather than inflicting losses on others, it is never praiseworthy to spare third parties by letting down the legitimate interests of someone one has pledged oneself to protect. Discretionary oughts should not be honoured vicariously. A trustee is obligated to press every claim the principal is entitled to press, and while the principal is also free to renege legitimate claims, the trustee is not, save by the principal's permission.

Here lies a divergence between first-person morality and the rules of vicarious action that comes in addition to the divergence that was established by the weak thesis of non-equivalence. The argument of the previous paragraph points towards the moderate thesis of non-equivalence, implying that the least urgent considerations of first-person behaviour – considerations of nobility, generosity and self-abnegation – must be set aside when an obligation of trusteeship comes into the picture. This is an aspect of the reduced right of a trustee to consider other factors than the interests of his principal. It may be called the ban on vicarious supererogatory action. Its existence proves that there is something to the moderate thesis.

Let us look at the ban on vicarious supererogatory action in the context of foreign policy. Are governments, like trustees in general, wrong to do things that their principals would be admired for doing but have no duty to do? Hans Morgenthau thinks so.

> The individual may say for himself: "*Fiat justitia, pereat mundus* (Let justice be done, even if the world perish)", but the state has no right to say so in the name of those who are in its care. Both individual and state must judge political action by universal moral principles, such as that of liberty. Yet while the individual has a moral right to sacrifice himself in defense of such a moral principle, the state has no right to let its moral disapprobation of the infringement of liberty get in the way of successful political action, itself inspired by the moral principle of national survival. (Morgenthau 1968, p. 10)

Morgenthau's view seems sensible. Few, if anyone, would deny that political leaders have no right to put "national survival" at risk for the sake of furthering other people's liberty. Nothing can prevent a person from sacrificing his own life to save others from oppression, but a political leader must not let national citizens pay for his righteousness with their lives.

Again, we must add the proviso that sacrifices will be justified if they have the approval of citizens. A government does nothing wrong in going beyond the call of duty if doing so gives expression to the moral ideals of citizens. If, for example, these are conveyed through the electoral process, they must be taken into account. But on many occasions, citizens have no simple way of communicating their ideals and the government no way of finding out whether supererogatory action would be countenanced or not. There may simply not be enough time for such communication to take place before a decision has to be made. What should the government do then? Two answers are conceivable. The first is that a government should not renounce legitimate national claims unless the citizens explicitly permit it to do so. This is in line with what has been said so far about political trusteeship. The second answer is that a government should do what it believes the citizens would have done if they had had the opportunity to state an explicit position. If, in particular, the national leadership has good reason to believe that people embrace certain ideals, then these ideals are its proper guideline. As a trustee, it should not only further national interests, but also represent national morality.

The second answer opens the door to unauthorized supererogatory action. It permits a government to pursue moral ideals without express public permission to do so. I shall call it the *permissive argument*. It relaxes the ban on vicarious supererogatory action, but its practical implications are largely indeterminate. The point is that political leaders will often be uncertain of what people want them to do in the absence of an explicit mandate, and the permissive argument does not tell how to deal with this kind of uncertainty. Which is the proper presumption – that citizens are generally disinclined go beyond the call of duty, or that they are inclined to do so? According to R.S. Downie (1964), it is the latter. He asks, in particular, if a government ought to devote national resources to helping victims of a natural disaster in another country and offers two reasons why it should. First, if "the government should prove too generous with public money or services to other countries the public can, at least in a liberal-democratic country, express its disapproval in a general election" (op.cit., p. 130). Second, governments "more often underrate than overrate thc moral sense of their electorate" (ibid.). Together, the permissive argument and Downie's argument all but annul the ban on vicarious supererogatory action. They suggest that political leaders should be particularly concerned not to press a legitimate national claim too hard. It would be wrong to do so if citizens take a more concessionary attitude, and there is greater risk of deflating than inflating their willingness to make concession. Hence, supererogatory action is compatible with the moral principles of trusteeship.

In my view, this challenge to the ban on supererogatory action does not stand up to closer scrutiny. Its basic premise – the permissive argument – fails to distinguish the two mistakes a government may make as far as supererogation is concerned. One mistake is to perform a supererogatory action that citizens disapprove of, the other is not to perform an action that has popular approval. The permissive argument puts the two mistakes on an equal footing, saying that a government should endeavour not to err in either way. It is worse, however, to err on the side of too little care for legitimate national interests than to err by doing too much. This is clearly the case when primary interests, like security or sovereignty, are at stake, but it may also be said more generally that a special responsibility for national citizens entails a special reason not to renege on claims that citizens may legitimately uphold.

To conclude, a government should not act on a discretionary ought, engaging in generosity or saintly and heroic acts on behalf of those who trust it to care for their interests. People may decide for themselves not to press legitimate national claims, and they may be praiseworthy for doing so, but political leaders cannot rightfully do this on their behalf, save by explicit permission.

Does the moderate thesis of non-equivalence stop here, or does it involve further reductions of the reasons of action that weigh with a trustee? Can we, more specifically, go beyond the ban on vicarious supererogatory action to establish an even stronger version of the moderate thesis of non-equivalence? Are there moral considerations that do not bear on vicarious action although they have straightforward practical implications for first-person behaviour? If there are, it will be a question of requirements that have enough normative force to generate non-discretionary oughts, but still are outweighed by the special obligation of trusteeship. They will relate neither to supererogatory actions nor to actions that all agents, acting for themselves or others, have reason to perform, but to actions of a third, intermediate kind. Do such third category considerations exist? I doubt it because I do not see how their existence can be established. Apart from the distinction between discretionary oughts and non-discretionary requirements, no threshold of moral urgency suggests itself.

7 Non-equivalence and moral indeterminacy

Starting from Nagel's idea that the special obligations of political leaders reduce their right to consider other factors than the national interest, we have so far found that political leaders must pursue national interests in a rational manner and not engage in supererogation. The nest two sections will extend the moderate thesis of non-equivalence by pointing out other ways in which vicarious action diverges from first-person behaviour.

Some situations of choice are *morally indeterminate* as far as first-person considerations are concerned. In such situations, no definite answer can be given to the question of what, all things considered, ought to de done. To be sure, not everyone believes that things are ever like this. The existence of moral indeterminacy is no foregone conclusion, and some philosophers rule it out (Hare 1979, ch. 2). It is not, they say, that moral considerations cannot *appear* to be pit against one another in irresolvable opposition, but there will always be an action that, upon close and sustained scrutiny, proves preferable from a moral point of view. Others believe, however, that some practical questions have no definite answer. Susan Wolf (1992, p. 788) writes:

> If … there is a plurality of values or principles or reasons for favoring and disfavoring things that does not form a complete well-ordered system, then it seems reasonable to expect that the realm of moral facts will contain pockets of indeterminacy. There will be cases in which there are good reasons for one position and good reasons for an incompatible position and no further overarching principle and perspective from which these can be put into any further overarching balance. In such cases, one might say that both positions are equally right. Or one might say that there is no right answer, no fact of the matter about what is right.

The discussion of chapter 1 suggests, indeed, that moral thinking revolves around a plurality of values or principles that do not form a well-ordered system. Hence, the expectation that we will come across pockets of indeterminacy seems well-grounded. One such situation has particular interest for our purpose. Assume that an agent faces a choice between two options, one of which would have adverse implications for himself, the other equally adverse implications for others. Nothing in the alternatives themselves recommends either before the other. What should then be done? It makes a difference for our assessment of this situation whether the choice is to be made by someone on his own behalf or in the capacity of a trustee. Looking beyond the alternatives in search of normative clues, nothing catches the eye in a first-person perspective, but in the case of vicarious action, one notes the special obligation that goes with trusteeship. If it is no worse, morally speaking, to favour a principal than to let him down, then favouring him is the course which naturally suggests itself. It is best in the light of all relevant factors, which in the case of vicarious action include more than factors pertaining to the alternatives as such. Thus, first-person assessment does not carry over without modification to vicarious action. There is, in other words, an element of indeterminacy in the picture.

This will be called the *indeterminacy justification of partiality*. When a trustee does not know for sure what is right and what is wrong, he should do what is best for the principal. Indeterminacy justifies, in particular, national favouritism. Like other elements of non-equivalence, this, too, comes with a qualification. Things should always be the way the principal wants, and there is no rationale of partiality in a situation of indeterminacy if a trustee is instructed by his principal not to be partial. The indeterminacy justification of favouritism applies only in the absence of such instruction.

Consider a government that can promote primary national interests only in ways adversely affecting the interests of foreign people. Should it do what is best for national citizens or rather sacrifice their interests to those of the foreigners in question? It will be torn between two considerations: the national obligation and a concern about the world at large. The former calls for the promotion of national interests; the latter implies that certain ways of promoting these interests are illegitimate. The two considerations must be compared to find out which is weightiest, and there are three logically possible results of this comparison: (1) the national obligation overrides the concern about foreigners; (2) the concern about foreigners overrides the national obligation; or (3) neither consideration overrides the other, i.e., the government has no basis for saying which is weightiest. Case (3) is an example of moral indeterminacy. If citizens are deciding for themselves how to resolve a problem like (3), no solution suggests itself as the best or most justified choice. If, by contrast, the choice is in the hands of political leaders who are not instructed by the citizens to act against national interests, then these interests come first.

This conclusion ties in with considerations of accountability. When a person sacrifices his own interests to those of others, he need not explain his reasons to anyone. The question of accountability for first-person behaviour arises only if an agent decides to do a thing that adversely affects other people. Then he will have to answer for his actions to those who suffer its adverse effects. When it comes to vicarious action, the question of accountability is more involved. If, on the one hand, a government foregoes the fulfillment of national interests out of concern for other states or peoples, it must be prepared to explain its reasons for doing so to those who carry the costs of its policy. If, on the other hand, the government pursues national interests at the expense of other states' or peoples' interests, these states or peoples can demand an explanation. Only the latter requirement has a parallel in first-person morality; the former is unique to vicarious action. We may say that such action involves not only outward but also inward accountability, and it is arguable that the inward aspect matters most. A government is first and foremost accountable to national citizens who have put their trust in it. Such accountability is central to the responsibility which goes with positions of political leadership. If a government foregoes national interests and cannot explain why national interests somehow fall short of the interests of other states with respect to normative force, it does not live up to its obligations as trustee. To be sure, even foreigners can demand an explanation when their interests are set aside, but the inward aspect of accountability is most pressing. After all, a government is not just an administrative agency that controls a certain territory; it is the government of a particular people and should answer to national citizens before anyone else.

A special case of moral indeterminacy, and an especially malignant case, is a *tragic dilemma*.

> Tragic dilemmas are those in which the agent has to choose between two actions, both of which are right in a way that makes it wrong to be indifferent between which is chosen. Normal dilemmas are those where the value of each choice is more or less the same as that of the other ... so that one is right whichever choice one makes. ... In tragic dilemmas, by contrast, whichever choice one makes one does a wrong. This is because one's failure to make the first choice cannot be compensated (at all, let alone in kind) by one's having made the other. (Dancy 1993, p. 123)

In a tragic dilemma, two sets of moral considerations stand opposed in what we may call a tragic conflict. Both are urgent, and neither outweighs the other. The choice is best described as an existential one: doing one thing rather than another serves to define what kind of person one is. It is not the kind of choice moral theory can help us to resolve. The intellectual process of balancing competing considerations to arrive at a conclusive judgment has come to a standstill. This is all there is to say about tragic dilemmas as far as first-person behaviour is concerned. True, we may investigate the proper attitude to existential choices, but no determinate rule of right action is available. When it comes to vicarious action, however, more can be said. The reasons that weigh upon someone who has to tackle a tragic dilemma on his own behalf are not equivalent to the reasons that weigh upon a trustee. The latter has no right to act on moral considerations that stand in a relation of tragic conflict to the care of his principal. If two alternatives are supported by urgent and equally strong reasons, the trustee should choose the one that caters best to the interest of the principal, resolving the tragic conflict in his favour.

In the literature on international relations, one often comes across arguments alluding to tragic dilemmas. An example is Dean Acheson's reflections upon the decision he faced in 1949, as advisor to President Truman, of "whether and with what degree of urgency to press the attempt to produce a thermonuclear weapon":

> A respected colleague advised me that it would be better that our whole nation and people should perish rather than be party to a course so evil as producing that weapon. I told him that on the Day of Judgment his view might be confirmed and that he was free to go forth and preach the necessity for salvation. It was not, however, a view which I could entertain as a public servant. (Acheson 1967, p. 13)

Granted the description Acheson's colleague gives of the case, it has the appearance of a tragic dilemma. To produce thermonuclear weapons is said to be an "evil course" and the same goes for not producing them, which allegedly puts the survival of nation and people at stake. Thus, both alternatives seem wrong, and moral considerations stand opposed in a tragic conflict. If so, Acheson's reply to his colleague is in line with the principle of partiality defended above.

A problem with this case is, however, that neither producing nor not producing thermonuclear weapons are actions that have immediate and unavoidable consequences for national citizens or other people. What Acheson and his colleague consider are alternatives that *risk* bringing evil or causing the nation to perish. Neither course of actions is certain to have adverse consequences. I shall look at this complication in the next section.

8 Risky policy

The epistemological circumstances of political choice are frequently imperfect. Factual uncertainty often surrounds the conduct of foreign policy. Thus, a government may suspect that the nation will suffer serious set-backs unless some defensive measure is taken, and this measure may in turn have very adverse effects on foreigners. Should it be taken? I shall call this the problem of *risky policy*. It raises the question of whether or not a government can defend primary national interests by harmful means that may turn out to be dispensable.

Let me start again with a brief remark about the simpler case of interpersonal trusteeship. It would be admirable for a person to risk his life rather than killing someone who just possibly posed a fatal threat to him. He is not, however, morally obligated to tolerate high risks in this respect. Doing so would be a supererogatory action on his part. This implies that a trustee, in a similar situation, should give those who are in his care the benefit of doubt unless he is explicitly instructed to act otherwise. He is morally required not to let them suffer high risks. It is worse to jeopardize the urgent interests of a principal than people who have no special claim on him. This will be called the principle of *partiality in decision under ignorance.*

This principle carries over to foreign policy. Some threats to primary national interests are obvious and unambiguous, but many are uncertain and subject to divergent assessments. The steps a state should take to protect such interests "are not fixed by nature nor identifiable by any generally accepted standard of objective criteria", but "are instead the products of fallible human judgment" (Brodie 1973, p. 343). Thus, a government may err in its beliefs about the prerequisites of national security, doing too much or too little. If it does too much, other states and peoples may suffer unnecessary harm; if it does too little, it risks sacrificing national survival. The argument above implies that political leaders should take particular care not to do too little. The nation has precedence if a government can avoid harm to foreigners only by running substantial risk of, say, military attack, terrorism or political subversion.

The principle of partiality in decision under ignorance is indeterminate in an important respect. The notion of high or substantial risk to primary national interests is ambiguous, and political rhetorics encourage inflated conceptions of what a nation needs to survive. Arnold Wolfers (1962, p. 59) says that a "nationalistic scale of values" has wide currency, and on this scale, the protection of any national economic asset or legal right is taken "to justify the sacrifice of almost every other value whether it be life, generosity, humane treatment of others, truthfulness, or obedience to the law" (ibid.). Moreover, it is sometimes held that states face constant threats to their existence. According to Stanley Hoffmann (1981, p. 47), "the international system is one which raises problems of survival incessantly", and Marshall Cohen (1984, p. 299) speaks of the "alarming degree" to which "the history of international relations is a history of selfishness and brutality". The international system emerges, in short, as a "precarious environment" (Sterling 1965, p.

259). Together, the tendencies to inflate vital interests and magnify risks may make the principle of partiality in decision under ignorance extensionally equivalent to the absolute priority principle. In view of this danger, it should be underlined that permissions of partiality must be established from case to case. There is no presumption to the effect that governments always have the right to act without restraint.

9 Conclusion

This chapter offers an answer to the question of how far a government may accord priority to national interests in the conduct of foreign policy. First, I rejected the idea that primary national interests pertaining to security, integrity and prosperity take precedence over every competing moral consideration. Then I argued that obligations of trusteeship warrant a somewhat greater concern about national interests on the part of political leaders than citizens would be justified in paying these interests if they were defending them on their own behalf. This extra measure of partiality can be summed up in four principles.

In the first place, the least urgent considerations of first-person behaviour – those that underlie supererogatory behaviour – must be set aside when the obligation of trusteeship comes into the picture. Thus, a government has no right to act on such considerations unless it has explicit instructions from the citizens to do so. This was called the ban on vicarious supererogatory action.

In the second place, in situations of moral indeterminacy, a trustee should take particular care to pay enough attention to the interests of the principal. When, in particular, political leaders cannot tell for sure what is right and what is wrong, they should do what is best for the nation. This was called the indeterminacy justification of partiality.

In the third place, a trustee is required not to let the principal suffer high risks of harm. This is the principle of partiality in decision under ignorance. It implies that a government must not jeopardize the urgent interests of national citizens even if this can only be avoided by doing things that risk harming foreigners.

Finally, a trustee must not let frivolous reasons enter into his deliberations. An agent is free to act non-optimally when he acts on his own behalf, but if he acts on behalf of another, he must do what he can to follow an optimal course of action. The role of trustee merges morality and rationality so that the latter becomes part of the former. This is to say that a government is obligated to pursue rational policies.

4 Morality and International Law

1 Introduction

Among the things a state can do to further national interests, acts of force have always been of particular concern. International war brings out in a pronounced way the disquieting aspects of unrestrained pursuit of national interests.[19] Hersch Lauterpacht (1946, p. 36) writes:

> It is not the dagger or the poison of the hired assassin or the sharp practice of the realistic politician which expresses most truly, upon final analysis, the ideas of '*raison d'état*'. It is the infliction, without a shadow of a specific right and without a claim to any particular right, of the calamities and indignities of war and of the territorial mutilation and the very annihilation of statehood following upon defeat in war.

The rest of this book deals with moral and legal problems pertaining to international conflict that involves (or may involve) acts of force. I will discuss both the legitimacy of war, as judged by standards of morality, and its legality.

There is a long tradition of thought on these issues. Theories of *just war*, developed by theologians, philosophers and legal theorists, share a framework of questions and categories that reveal a remarkable conceptual continuity through time. All along, normative standards have divided into two categories: principles of *jus ad bellum* which spell out aims and occasions that warrant resort to force, and principles of *jus in bello* which specify rules of warfare, i.e., restrictions on what a government and its armed forces may do to defeat an adversary during hostilities. This chapter begins with a brief retrospect of classical, medieval and early modern doctrines of *jus ad bellum* (section 2). I am not, however, concerned with the history of just war theory as such. Theorists of antiquity, the Middle Ages and the Renaissance have an interest because they define a lasting agenda and anticipate important contemporary positions. In the modern world, just war theory developed into international law of armed conflict, and the chapter continues with a discussion of the specific character of international law as a legal system (section

3). Finally, it offers some general observations on the relationship between morality and law, stressing the role of pragmatic considerations in translating moral principles into legal rules (section 4).

2 An historical retrospect of just war theory

Philosophical investigation of just and unjust war is as old as political theory in Europe. It was not, to be sure, a dominant preoccupation of philosophers in antiquity, but both Plato and Aristotle gave serious thought to it, as did Augustine.

In Aristotle's view, states should not engage in military action for any purpose, only to attain objectives that warrant such drastic measures. He goes on to distinguish between two warrants of war. There are, in the first place, *defensive* justifications that refer to wrongs which may (or even must) be averted or punished by means of force. Aristotle counts resistance to conquest in this category. The object of military training is, he says, "not to bring into subjection those not deserving of such treatment, but to enable men … to save themselves from becoming subject to others" (Aristotle 1986, 1333b37; p. 435). This is the first assertion of a right to take up arms in *self-defence*. It is not the only defensive warrant we will hear about, but it certainly receives the greatest and most sustained attention. In the second place, there are *offensive* justifications of war. They divide into several sub-categories, some of which will be discussed in chapter 7. It is sometimes argued that states are allowed or required to undertake war with a view to transforming or reforming the social or political institutions and arrangements of foreign countries. This plea figures prominently in Aristotle's argument. He holds that an object of military training, besides self-defence, is "to enable men … to win a position of leadership, exercised for the benefit of the ruled" (ibid.).

Augustine's writings on just war are directed against the widespread conviction among early Christians that participation in war is always sinful. His main contention is that Christ's command not to resist evil – "if any one strike thee on the right cheek, turn to him the left also" – does not sanction pacifism. According to the pacifist position, whether of religious inspiration or grounded in secular morality, acts of force are always wrong. This is the antithesis of the entire just war tradition. Augustine challenges it by saying that Christ's request to turn the other cheek concerns "not a bodily action, but an inward disposition", and a "great deal depends on the causes for which men undertake wars" (Augustine 1962, ch. 22, pp. 166 and 165). The crucial test is that violence is divinely endorsed: "When war is undertaken in obedience to God … it must be allowed to be a righteous war" (ibid.).

Augustine argues, in particular, that Christians should see to it that political authorities everywhere root out ungodly conduct. Thus, "wars might be waged by the good, in order that, by bringing under the yoke the unbridled lusts of men, those vices might be abolished which ought, under a just government, to be either extirpated or suppressed" (Augustine 1962a, pp. 179–180). It is a question of forcible intervention aimed at spiritual reform – the eradication of sin and the conversion of sinners. Augustine is in no doubt that great benefits ensue from such intervention. He is confident that "the person from whom is taken away the freedom which he abuses in doing wrong is vanquished with benefit to himself; since nothing is more truly a misfortune than that good fortune of offenders, by which pernicious impunity is maintained, and the evil disposition, like the enemy within the man, is strengthened" (ibid., p. 179).

These remarks inaugurate the preoccupation of Christian theorists with *holy war*. The notion enjoys a surge of interest during the Middle Ages. It provides the doctrinal backing of a church at the apex of its spiritual and worldly power, intent on spreading the faith beyond its European stronghold and regaining the Holy Land from the Muslims. Christian thinkers from Augustine to the Renaissance stress this offensive warrant of war, and are sometimes far more reluctant to justify defensive use of deadly force. Thus, Thomas Aquinas vacillates between an unconditional right of self-defence and a highly circumscribed permission to kill aggressors only if the "public good" calls for it, with "private animosity" playing no part in the killing (Ramsey 1961, pp. 35–42).

The religious warrant of offensive war reflected a more basic conception of the Christian world as a transnational community, united by allegiance to the same confessional dogmas. This conception did not only find expression in philosophical theories, it was also to some extent rooted in international realities. The Church of Rome frequently asserted its will against local, secular rulers during the High Middle Ages. Both the notion of holy war and the disregard of sovereignty made good sense in practical terms. The ideological hegemony and worldly power of the medieval Church provided an institutional framework for the interpretation and implementation of just war principles. This went a long way in allaying the risk that any prince who saw fit could forcibly secure some advantage under religious pretext. Inis Claude Jr. (1980, p. 88) writes:

> The idea of a judge standing above the prince was by no means unthinkable. Indeed, the church, which provided the doctrine, also provided the judge and the sanctions. Christendom thought it had a consensus on the nature of justice, and it had an authoritative interpreter of the moral law. ... One ought not to conclude that the doc-

> trine of just war was systematically implemented, but neither should one believe that the idea of applying the doctrine to the affairs of the real world seemed quite so improbable then as it does now.

When the inspiration of orthodox Christianity waned, just war theory underwent a significant reorientation. The main transitory character is the Spanish theologian Franciscus de Victoria. His major works, *De Indis* (On Indians) and *De jure belli* (On the Law of War), date from 1532. They were intended for the very practical purpose of curbing Spanish conduct in the recently conquered colonies of the New World, but had lasting theoretical implications. Victoria introduces two radical innovations. First, he discards the confessional premises of medieval philosophy in favour of a predominantly secular perspective on politics. The most conspicuous victim of this reorientation is the notion of holy war. Victoria flatly asserts that "[d]ifference of religion is not a cause of just war" (quoted in Johnson 1981, p. 95). He acknowledges only defensive warrants that cite mundane wrongs inflicted on tangible interests.

> He stresses that wars are justified only when fault exists that can be known by natural reason, and to clarify this he mentions various kinds of self-defense: the right to oppose pillage, rape, and killing. Elsewhere he treats the right of free passage as known from nature, justifying the free, peaceful passage of missionaries and traders among the Indians and declaring that the Spanish may make war to enforce this free passage. (Johnson 1981, p. 97)

The last sentence reflects a medieval vestige in Victoria's thought. He takes the right of self-defence to authorize military action on behalf of missionaries on foreign soil. But there is no question of converting pagans by the sword. All in all, the argument has great affinity to contemporary conceptions of self-defence.

Victoria's second radical innovation in just war theory is related not so much to substantive principle as to his wider political outlook. He was strongly opposed to the aspirations of emperor Charles V, in the middle of the 16th century, to consolidate and extend Habsburg rule in Europe and beyond. The notion of *sovereignty* lies at the heart of Victoria's thinking. He sees the right to use violence when a just cause exists as an essential ingredient of political independence and is thus the first just war theorist to take the existence of a multi-state system for granted (Elbe 1939, p. 674). The notion that any right of war belongs equally to the government of each state is sometimes challenged by later writers, but after Victoria it has had the onus of proof on its side.

Victoria's rejection of holy war and his emphasis on state sovereignty are related developments in just war thinking. Both bear witness to the dismantling, ideologically as well as politically, of the world of medieval Christendom. Political authorities were no longer seen primarily as servants of a higher cause. From now on, their responsibilities were mainly mundane. Rather than act on supernatural directives, they should pursue the material advantage of their subjects.[20]

The new conception of political morality finds its first clear expression in Hugo Grotius' *De jure belli ac pacis* (The Law of War and Peace). Written during the Thirty Years War and published in 1625, it reflects the influence of Renaissance secularization. Grotius discounts all religiously inspired warrants of war, being convinced that neither paganism nor impurity of faith call for Christian crusade. His conception of *jus ad bellum* is austere, restrictionist and conservative, permitting military means to be used solely for the defence of established rights, and then only if their use is confidently believed to be a necessary expedient (Bull 1966, pp. 55–56). Among established rights, territorial integrity and political sovereignty stand out. The defence of borders and independence is, in Grotius' view, the most obvious warrant of war.

De jure belli ac pacis inaugurates the modern law of nations or *international law*. Grotius divides it into three sub-categories: one part is principles "derived from nature" (which means that they are justified by philosophical argument), another is "divine ordinances" and a third is law which has "its origin in custom and tacit agreement" (Grotius [1625] 1970, para. 1, p. 39). The latter is positive law – rules that "the agreement of nations has established" (para. 26, p. 52). As Terry Nardin (1983, p. 59) points out, theologians and philosophers of the early modern period, Grotius included, at first invoke the idea of a distinct body of agreement-based law "only fleetingly". It is not until the late 18th century that positive conventions take on major importance. The turning point is the appearance of compilations of treaties and diplomatic codes, collected and edited by jurists who set little store by the philosophical and theological credentials of the rules they recorded. Thus, the series of compendia published by the German scholar and politician Georg Friedrich von Martens, beginning in 1790 and continuing after his death, gave tangible expression to the idea that international law "summarized the rules that might be distilled from state practice … for the use of statesmen and scholars seeking more precise knowledge of international legal practice" (ibid., p. 64).

3 International law

As a legal system, international law differs significantly from the legal systems of individual states. Some believe, indeed, that the term "international law" is a misnomer. Legal positivists hold that normative principles have legal status only if they are backed up by an effective threat of punishment for disobedience. The foremost representative of this view, John Austin, speaks of laws as "commands" that "proceed from superiors", and "superiority" is defined as "might: the power of affecting others with evil and pain, and of forcing them, through fear of that evil, to fashion their conduct to one's wishes" (Austin [1832] 1954, p. 24; italics deleted).

If we accept Austin's "command theory", there is much to be said for the view that international law is no true legal system. The institutional weaknesses of the international legal order are all too obvious. Thus, the international system lacks a legislative body from which rules and regulations emanate, and no single institution administers law on the basis of a unique and incontestable authority to adjudicate specific cases. International legislation and adjudication are in the hands of all states on an equal basis. There are no fixed procedures for resolving disagreement as to whether some norm has the status of law or how existing legal provisions are to be interpreted; nor is there any central enforcement agency. Still, there exists a body of normative principles that goes under the name of international law and play an undeniable role in debates and diplomatic negotiations about proper conduct in relations between states. Opinions differ, to be sure, on how important the role of these principles really is. Some think they contribute substantially in shaping foreign policy, others believe they are honoured only when the stakes are low or their prescriptions coincide with hard calculations of national interest.

Now, the extent of respect for international law is no constant of international life. It varies with the circumstances, and an important question is whether or not it somehow depends on the way legal rules are formulated. Can we, in particular, buttress the practical impact of such rules by design – making them more liable to place effective constraints on foreign policy? This pragmatic problem will be central to the discussion that follows. It has interest for those who think that international law plays an important role in international politics, as well as those who discount its current role but would like to boost its future importance. The present century has seen three changes that are relevant on this score.[21] In the first place, international law has become the law of all members of the international system, not only European states or the

"Christian world". In the second place, it has "hardened into an elaborate complex of institutions, organizations, precise prescriptions and juristic doctrines" (Niemeyer 1941, p. 5). One aspect of this is that there has grown up a formal machinery for the interpretation, elaboration and application of legal rules. Its most important contemporary component is the *United Nations*. International law lies at the heart of almost everything this organization does, in the General Assembly, in specialized organizations or throughout the large network of committees. Another aspect of this "hardening" process is that the interpretation and elaboration of international law long ceased to be a spare-time job of theologians and philosophers. These tasks have been taken over by a profession of its own, international jurists, who find employment as functionaries in international organizations as well as counsellors of national governments. In the third place, treaties between states have become by far the most important source of international legal rules. A treaty is, briefly put, a formal agreement entered into by the official and authorized representatives – and if necessary ratified by the legislatures – of two or more states. Treaties are one main constituent part of positive law as characterized above; the other is custom. The present century has, however, seen the supersession of the latter by the former through an "evergrowing practical application of explicit official agreement as a way of creating or demonstrating the norms of international law" (Lipson 1975, p. 419). A custom is a much more amorphous entity than a treaty. Its existence presupposes continued, concordant behaviour of a number of states in a certain kind of situation; this practice being also acquiesced in by other states, and confirmed by a competent international authority (D'Amato 1971, p. 7). When one speaks of custom in the legal sense, it is furthermore assumed that concordant behaviour is more than habitual behaviour. There must attach a sense of obligation to it. It goes without saying that customs will not always present themselves clearly and unambiguously to governments. Treaties, by contrast, almost always allow of a fairly straightforward identification. An international agreement exists if and only if its provisions and approval by the parties are on record.

This brief account of legal history challenges the earlier argument about the institutional weakness of the international legal order at a central point. The increasing role of positive international law makes the absence of a single, central legislature less of a problem. To be sure, the existence of positive law is not in itself enough to assuage all weaknesses. If treaties of conflicting contents are invoked, the problem of pinpointing authoritative legal provisions with accuracy may be just as great as it was when one had to rely on theological and philosophical interpretations of "natural law". But if a body of pivotal treaties emerges to become the predominant premise of judicial judgment, owing to a general recognition of their supreme legal status, then the situation is different. We will then have a functional equivalent of authoritative legislation. Although legal rules do not emanate from a single, universally recognized legislature, there will be broad agreement on their contents and consensus as to which provisions are relevant to which cases. As far as the law of military conflict is concerned, this functional equivalent of central legislation exists today. The *Charter* of the United Nations stands out as a pivotal treaty. It is the natural point of departure whenever the legality of military action becomes the object of assessment.

4 From moral principles to legal rules

The previous section shows that international law largely takes shape through a decentralized and uncoordinated process. States enter into agreements or start to behave in specific ways and as a result, treaties and customs arise. There is, accordingly, no central legislature to which proposals for revisions of existing law can be directed. Yet it makes good sense to ask if international law is as it ought to be – if, in particular, it lives up to moral standards.

Moral principles provide important premises for any discussion of what international law should be like, but legislation is different from moral thinking. There is, in particular, no saying that every part of morality should have a counterpart in law. Pragmatic arguments of various kinds can come into the picture and tell against translating moral principles into legal injunctions. I shall consider four such arguments.

In the first place, some moral principles may be thought incapable of becoming effective law. However strong their philosophical rationale, they should not guide legislation because they are unlikely to be acted upon to any great extent. This will be called the *irrelevance* argument. For an illustration of how it can be elaborated, consider Thomas Aquinas' objection to the idea that each element of "natural law" – his term for the true moral theory – should be reflected in "human" or positive law.

> The mere fact of a change in law itself can be adverse to the public welfare to some degree. This is because custom is very important in the observance of law since things done contrary to general custom, even if they are not important, are considered serious offenses. Therefore when a law is changed the restraining power of the law is

> lessened because custom is set aside. Therefore human law should never be changed unless the common welfare is compensated in some way for the harm done in that respect. (Aquinas 1988, question 97, p. 57)

Aquinas sees stability as a prerequisite of effective legislation, and denies that an established rule should be altered upon the first realization that it does not fully reflect the demands of morality. New rules will never be obeyed to the same extent as the injunctions they replace. Thus, a new legal rule that is preferable to established law from a purely moral point of view should be introduced only if it results in an improvement all things considered, i.e. considering both the improvement it will produce if its is obeyed and the likelihood that it will be obeyed. The moral quality of law must be balanced against its expected potential for influencing human behaviour.

In the second place, a new legal rule may have practical impact, but not the right kind of impact. Thus, an effort to improve social life through the introduction of new laws may turn out to make things worse. This will be called the *counterfinality* argument. It is invoked, for example, by those who say that radical ideas of a utopian bent will aggravate rather than ameliorate imperfect conditions if they are translated into law. The assumption is that they hold up impossible ideals which sap the motivational basis of established injunctions without putting anything in their place. Aquinas even advanced this argument in his discussion of the relationship between natural and human law. Alluding to a passage in the Gospel according to St. Matthew, he warns that the introduction of very demanding legal rules may bring the entire legal edifice into disrepute.

> 'if they pour new wine' – that is, prescriptions of perfect behaviour – 'into old wineskins' – that is, imperfect persons – 'then the wineskins will break, and the wine is spilled' – which is to say that the prescriptions will fall into disrepute, and as a result thereof people will degenerate to become even worse than they were. (Aquinas 1967, question 96, p. 132)

This is a controversial assumption – an axiom to conservatives and a self-serving prejudice to political radicals. I shall not, however, go into substantive issues of the sociology of law at this point. Whatever its merits in concrete cases, legal conservatism exemplifies the general idea that legal reforms can worsen the things they were meant to improve.

In the third place, some moral principles may be unfit for incorporation in law because legal rules corresponding to these principles will be too vague to yield determinate conclusions about what conduct they permit. This is clearly problematic if the conduct whose legal status they leave indeterminate is illegitimate or otherwise undesirable. If so, one may fear that people will use the rules in question as cloaks of illegal and unwanted behaviour, or that they will act wrongly in the belief that what they do is legally permissible. David Hume stresses this problem in his discussion of the law of property. Many rules might, he says, serve the purpose of separating possessions so as to ensure that society is not torn asunder by conflict over scarce material resources, but which is it to be?

> We shall suppose that a creature, possessed of reason but unacquainted with human nature, deliberates with himself what rules of justice or property would best promote public interest, and establish peace and security among mankind: His most obvious thought would be, to assign the largest possessions to the most extensive virtue, and give every one power of doing good, proportioned to his inclination. In a perfect theocracy, where a being, infinitely intelligent, governs by particular volitions, this rule would certainly have place, and might serve to the wisest purposes: But were mankind to execute such a law, so great is the uncertainty of merit, both from the natural obscurity, and from the self-conceit of each individual, that no determinate rule of conduct would ever result from it; and the total dissolution of society must be the immediate consequence. (Hume [1777] 1975, p. 193)

Hume's point is that the principle "to each according to virtue" is too imprecise to determine which possessions various persons are entitled to. There will be both genuine uncertainty about relative merit and a fair amount of special pleading aimed at dressing up illegitimate demands as claims from virtue. As a result, the principle in question will afford no basis for settling material conflicts. Even if it does not have the "total dissolution of society" as its immediate consequence, it is liable to become a pretext of many efforts to appropriate what rightfully belongs to others. This line of argument can be stated more generally: One should beware of legal rules that do not yield determinate rules of conduct and may therefore serve as pretexts of illegitimate behaviour. A valid moral principle is unfit to become part of the law if it cannot be translated into a reasonably precise statute. In Hume's words, "a rule, which, in speculation, may seem the most advantageous to society, may yet be found, in practice, totally pernicious and destructive" (ibid.). This will be called the *vagueness* argument.

In the fourth place, pragmatic concerns about the relationship between moral principles and law can take the form of a so-called *slippery slope* argument. The general structure of this argument is as follows: (1) If X is permitted, Y will be hard to avoid; (2) Y is morally unacceptable or otherwise undesirable; therefore (3) X must not be permitted.[22] The crux of the argument is premise (1), which postulates that a slippery slope exists. The nature of this slope – the mechanism that renders Y unavoidable if X is permitted – may differ from one case to another. Thus, there are different versions of the slippery slope argument. One says that ascribing a normative predicate, P, to an object that possesses the attributes $a_1, a_2, a_3, \ldots a_n$, inevitably implies that P will also be ascribed to objects that possess only the attributes $a_1, a_2, a_3, \ldots a_{n-1}$. Here is an illustration: If public support is given to French language schools in Norway because they cannot support themselves economically and are a source of valuable cultural impulses, then the extension of public support even to uneconomic schools of other foreign languages is inevitable. The normative predicate is "deserving of public support", and among foreign language schools, only the French have all the meritorious attributes, but because others share some such attributes (teaching a foreign language, being uneconomical), it is unavoidable that public support be extended to them as well. If we add that the latter is undesirable because the total costs will be excessive, we have a slippery slope argument against public support to French language schools.[23]

Another version of the slippery slope argument says that certain combinations of legal rules give rise to legal codes that are unstable in the sense that people who accept and act on one rule contained in such a code, will be disinclined to act on another, but rather favour its abolition. In this case, we land on the slippery slope because of psychological factors. Gregory Trianosky (1978, p. 419) says that "certain combinations of rules might generate internal stresses or conflicts in moral agents and ... such psychological stresses might seriously affect the probabilities of their acting as the code required or recommended." In general, two provisions, L_1 and L_2, cannot both be effective rules of conduct in a given legal code if L_1 fosters attitudes that undermine respect for L_2. People who come to accept L_1 as a valid requirement will find it hard to countenance L_2 and vice versa.

These four pragmatic arguments set the stage for a discussion of the relationship between moral principles and international law. The task is to make legal rules reflective of moral concerns and at the same time to ensure that they are causally effective and productive of the right effects. This problem has preoccupied legal theorists ever since they began to see the international system as a system of independent, territorial states whose external objectives are basically secular. The Italian jurist Alberico Gentili, who taught law at Oxford at the end of the sixteenth century, was the first theorist to discard the purely philosophical perspective on just war in favour of practical jurisprudence. He "differs from his predecessors by a keen sense of realism which derives inspiration from human nature and concrete facts rather than abstract principles and metaphysical assumptions" (Elbe 1939, p. 677). Yet his writings are perhaps most important for the example they set to Grotius, who attacks head on those who hold the "law of war and peace" in contempt as "having no reality outside of an empty name" (Grotius [1625] 1970, para. 3, p. 39). This is, he says, to ignore the many motives and dispositions that facilitate compliance with morality and law, such as "man's inclination toward sociableness", the "torments and anguish" which follow upon the commitment of injustice, and the prudential consideration that "all things are uncertain the moment men depart from peace" (par. 14, p. 46; par. 20, p. 49; par. 22, p. 50). Thus, Grotius finds many moral motives in human nature, and it comes as no surprise that he sees no need for pragmatic concessions in translating just war principles into legal provisions. He feels compelled, however, to meet the skeptical challenge that "war is irreconcilable with all law" (ibid., par. 3, p. 40). His simplistic philosophical anthropology notwithstanding, he puts legal practicalities and pragmatic concerns firmly on the agenda. But his discussion of the relationship between morality and international law is unsystematic and incomplete, and the same goes for many later treatments of this subject. I hope to rectify that shortcoming.

5 The Right of National Self-Defence

1 Introduction

It is widely thought that a state is morally justified in defending its borders and sovereignty by means of force. Some, however, deny this, and their view must be taken seriously.

The morality of national self-defence brings up problems that relate closely to the question of whether or not an individual who is attacked by harmful means may respond in kind. I shall therefore start with that question, arguing in section 2 that individuals have a moral right of self-defence. Section 3 proceeds to show that this right has an analogy in a right of national self-defence. Then sections 4 and 5 will confront two forceful arguments to the effect that the right of national self-defence is generally overridden by, respectively, consequentialist and deontological considerations. Neither argument can be confidently dismissed, but both may be set aside on the ground that governments are first and foremost responsible for furthering national interests in situations of moral conflict or when problems of risky policy arise.

2 The individual right of self-defence

Can a person on whom harm is about to be inflicted defend himself by means of force, granted that this is a necessary means of defence? Doing harm was defined, in chapter 1, as doing things that cause other people's death, mutilation or incapacitation, and actions of such effects may be called *lethal aggression*. Most people answer the question above by claiming that there exists a right of defending oneself against lethal aggression. This is to say that doing harm is justified if it is a necessary means of resisting harmful conduct. I shall examine this idea in detail.

Several questions must be answered before the common belief that people have a right of self-defence can become a determinate principle of right action. First, what kind of harm may be inflicted in response to lethal aggression? Second, what does the proviso of necessity – the stipulation that doing harm must be a necessary means of defence – amount to? I think these questions boil down to one. People tend to believe that a victim of lethal aggression is allowed to protect himself by every necessary means, which is to say that no type of harmful conduct can written off as impermissible *per se*. It all depends on which measures are needed in the situation. Thus, I am not allowed to hurt or kill an aggressor if I can protect myself equally well, or at least adequately, by hiding from his assault, but if there is nowhere to hide and no non-violent way of stopping the assault, I may resort to force. I should not, however, kill the aggressor if shooting him in the leg would suffice for my defence. Can the proviso of necessity be spelled out in more general terms? It may mean several things: that harmful measures are justified only if they are the only available resort, or the only effective way of preventing harm, or the resort that has the highest probability of succeeding. As the choice between means of defence must often be made under great stress, there can be no question of defining necessity so subtly that no victim of aggression can be expected to go through the relevant deliberations. Still, for the proviso to make any practical difference, it must place real constraints on permissible behaviour. Consider, by way of contrast, Thomas Hobbes' definition of the "right of nature" as "the Liberty each man hath, to use his own power, as he will himselfe, for the preservation of his own Nature; that is to say, his own Life; and consequently, of doing anything, which in his own Judgement, and Reason, he shall conceive to be the aptest means thereunto" (Hobbes [1651] 1975, ch. 14., p. 66). This is more than the proviso of necessity permits. The aptest means of defence need not be the only means with a good chance of arresting an attack. The importance of the proviso of necessity is that it compels us to ask if circumstances really are as they have to be before harm can be done in a given situation.

Third, what does it mean to say that a person enjoys a *right* of self-defence? It means that he is permitted to harm anyone who sets out to harm him. He has, in other words, no duty to abstain from doing so. Other people, however, have a duty not to hinder him from doing what he is permitted to do, by obstructing or otherwise interfering with his conduct.

Fourth, should the right of self-defence be narrowly construed to comprise only defence against an on-going attack, or does it have broader scope, justifying even pre-emptive attack when there is solid reason to believe that lethal aggression is imminent? This is a hard question that will be bracketed now to be raised again in chapter 6.

Fifth, does the right of self-defence relate to all kinds of lethal aggression? This question must be asked because harmful actions fall into two categories that seem quite different from a moral point of view. When harm is done for the deliberate purpose of killing or mutilating people, it is a case of *wilful* lethal aggression. This label covers actions that aim at harm either as a goal in itself or as a means to something else. They differ from the actions of people who do harm without wanting to, sometimes even unwittingly. An example of such *unintentional* lethal aggression is driving a car at full speed into a crowd of people after having suffered a heart attack and lost consciousness. The right of self-defence is definitely a right to defend oneself against wilful aggression, but does it permit harmful response to unintentional aggression, too? This problem is best deferred until the next question has been brought up: Is there really a right of self-defence?

While most people recognize a right of self-defence, some do not. Pacifists believe the use of violence – at least lethal violence – is never justified. I have already alluded to this view in chapter 3. It has received different justifications, religious and secular – far too many to record here. I shall confine myself to elaborating a general rebuttal of the pacifist position. John Locke asks how an "innocent" person who has no "settled design upon another man's life" is to act when someone challenges him to a struggle of life and death. He answers that it is "reasonable and just I should have a right to destroy that which threatens me with destruction; for by the fundamental law of Nature, man being to be preserved as much as possible, when all cannot be preserved, the *safety of the innocent is to be preferred*" (Locke [1690] 1984, sect. 16, p. 125; italics added). In other words, if it is virtually certain that life will be lost owing to someone's murderous design, then the would-be murderer has the weakest claim to survive. Religious fatalism aside, how could it possibly be thought that the murderer is more entitled to live or that there is no moral difference between his death and the death of his victim? The innocent is to be saved because his death is the greater evil; hence, a harmful response to harm is permitted when it is the only effective means of preventing harm to an innocent person.

When Locke speaks of a "settled design upon another man's life", he clearly has wilful aggression in mind. His argument grounds a permission to harm those who intend to harm other people, but it does not right away certify harm in response to unintentional aggression. Is the infliction of harm justified even in response to harm that is done unintentionally or even unwittingly? Is, in other words, the right of self-defence a right to defend oneself by any necessary means against all forms of lethal aggression? How far does the proper response to a harmful action depend on the aggressor's *fault* in performing it? While fault is clearly germane to moral problems of lethal aggression, it may not matter enough to make unintentional aggression safe from response in kind. Judith Jarvis Thomson (1991, p. 285) asserts that the fault of an aggressor "is not relevant when what is in question is his life for yours". How can this position be defended? It seems equivalent to saying, in a more precise rendering of Locke's phrase, that when all cannot be preserved, the safety of the *altogether* innocent is to be preferred. Thus, someone who unwittingly or unintentionally puts another person's life at stake, is technically speaking guilty of what takes place although he bears no moral responsibility for it. The other person, by contrast, is entirely free of fault. Thus, when a choice must be made, the unintentional aggressor has a (slightly) weaker claim to live.

I shall leave matters at that for the time being. The problem of fault in relation to lethal aggression returns in section 5. Until then, the right of self-defence is defined narrowly as a right that warrants harmful response to the wilful infliction of harm.

3 National self-defence

In the previous section, I described the right of self-defence as a right belonging to people who are victims of lethal aggression. It is widely assumed that there also exists a right of *national* self-defence. An analogy is drawn "between the individual's right to defend his physical person against unlawful acts of violence and the nation's right to protect its 'physical person', its territorial integrity, against similar acts" (Tucker 1960, pp. 123–124). Do nations – or, more accurately, states – have such a right?

Acts of violence that threaten the territorial integrity of a state may be of many kinds. They can be distinguished according to the dimension of military operations as well as the aim behind them. As far as dimension is concerned, limited commando raids are at one end of a continuum that has all-out invasion at the other. What I say below bears most directly on how a state may respond to the latter. Large-scale military encroachments have the strongest title to warrant forceful response under the license of a right of national self-defence.

When it comes to the aim of military action, distinctions must be drawn more carefully. External threats to territorial integrity may spring from different designs. First, they may amount to lethal aggression – military action aimed at killing, mutilating or incapacitating people. These clearly warrant military self-defence. Lethal aggression is no less serious in international relations than in relations between individuals. If foreign troops invade a country with a view to slaughtering people, national self-defence is literally nothing but personal self-defence writ large. To this extent, we may say that a state enjoys an "exact equivalent of a man's right to defend himself against another man" (Teichman

1986, p. 87). Rarely, however, have governments been called upon to defend citizens against outright lethal aggression. There are examples of states that have made it their objective to rain destruction on other states, but few invasions are initiated with human slaughter as their express or unmistakable purpose. However, another type of external threat is a commonplace in international relations: military encroachment aimed at political control – at most, annexation, at least, the replacement of one regime with another subservient to foreign interests. Such an action, although carried out by military means, poses no immediate threat to the lives of those who live in the countries under attack. It rather threatens their freedoms or political sovereignty and may be called *political aggression*. What will happen if effective resistance is not put up, is not death or mutilation, but a greater or lesser loss of civil and political liberties on the part of a greater or lesser number of people in the invaded state.

Is there a right of national self-defence against political aggression? Such defence has no obvious warrant in Locke's argument that the safety of the innocent should be preferred to the life of a would-be murderer. External encroachments aimed at political concessions need not lead to the loss of human lives unless the aggrieved state mobilizes to defend its borders and independence. The people of the invaded state are, to be sure, the innocent party in the conflict, but their safety is not obviously at stake, as everyone seems safe provided the invaded state does not defend its sovereignty by force.

In view of this, one may conclude that military self-defence is illegitimate in case of political aggression. A choice between the safety of the innocent and that of an aggressor is the only valid reason to take another person's life, and the protection of sovereignty and freedom involves no such choice. This argument, which denies that the right of national self-defence permits forceful response to political aggression, will be called the *negative argument*. Some who find it congenial may object that I have stated it too loosely. The objectionable thing about defence of sovereignty is not simply that life will be lost, but that so *many* lives will be taken before the attack is rebuffed. I shall, however, defer the question of numbers until later and start with an argument to the effect that *any* destruction of life is impermissible for the protection of freedoms and sovereignty.

The negative argument is suggested by Jeffrie Murphy, who has doubts about any attempt to "make moral capital" out of notions like national interests and national self-defence.

> [I]nsofar as the death of a state is not identical with the deaths of individual human beings, why is the death of a state a morally bad thing? … It is at least worth considering the possibility that the only moral problems arising in war are the oldest and most common and most important – namely, are human beings being hurt and killed, who are they, and why are they? (Murphy 1973, p. 539)

Alluding to Locke again, one may object to the negative argument that the safety of the innocent means more than his survival. Freedom, not just life as such, can be defended at the risk of killing aggressors. Bluntly put, the sovereignty of a state is to be preferred to the lives of invading soldiers. This will be called the *positive argument*. It endorses a national right to take up arms in defence of political sovereignty. I shall look at two justifications of it.

In the first place, one may go back to the question of legitimate self-defence in interpersonal relations and invoke an extended right of individual self-defence that entails the positive argument. Gregory Kavka (1984, p. 128) holds that "the right of self-defence applies to the preservation of the central values of one's life as well as to biological survival". Someone who remains intact *qua* "physical person" still dies in a significant sense if he loses the things that make his life distinctive and valuable to him. This is tantamount to saying that freedom is as important as survival, which suggests a broad conception of safety and an extended right of self-defence. An innocent person may resort to force not just in response to harmful assaults, but also to protect himself from imprisonment and suppression, and a state may do the same to protect citizens against lethal as well as political aggression.

In the second place, Locke himself suggests an extension of his argument about the safety of the innocent. This does not involve a broader conception of safety, but it still implies that states have a right of self-defence against political aggression.

> [I]t [is] lawful for a man to kill a thief who has not in the least hurt him, nor declared any design upon his life, any farther than by the use of force, so to get him in his power as to take away his money, or what he pleases from him; because using force, where he has no right to get me into his power, let his pretence be what it will, I have no reason to suppose that he who would take away my liberty would not, when he had me in his power, take away everything else. And, therefore, it is lawful for me to … kill him if I can; for to that hazard does he justly expose himself. (Locke [1690] 1984, sect. 18, p. 126)

The point is that someone who attempts to take away another's liberty or possessions is liable to do him physical harm as well. The victim's life will not be secure despite assurances to the contrary. This line of argument can be carried over from interpersonal to international relations. The risk to citizens whose country is under attack is not only that their freedoms will be lost, but even their lives, in greater or lesser numbers. History shows that political aggression has often brought gross violations of personal security in its train. Although genocide is a relatively rare occurrence, torture and executions frequently accompany the efforts of one state to acquire and consolidate political control over another. If people defend national borders by force, they therefore act within the right of self-defence against lethal aggression.

I do not think either justification of the positive argument will succeed in proving beyond doubt that there exists a right of national self-defence against political aggression. To the view that freedom is as important as survival, one may object that the loss of freedom, as opposed to the loss of life, is never irreversible. People may win back their sovereignty by non-violent means or through the many social forces that work against lasting political suppression. Thus, "it is arguable that, as long as situations offer options for non-lethal resistance, they confront the victim with a fate that is not as bad as being killed, and that such situations do, therefore, not provide a justification for self-defensive killing" (Roose 1990, p. 166). Moreover, one may object to the extension of Locke's thesis about the safety of the innocent that a *certain* loss of life in war is of more concern than a mere *risk* that life will be lost through future occupation by an aggressor state.

Yet, the positive argument has the majority on its side. Few people subscribe to the view that military means can only be legitimately employed in response to an external attack that is expressly or unmistakably aimed at murder and mutilation. Citing numbers in this way does not, to be sure, answer Murphy's question of whether the "death of a state" is really a bad thing unless it is "identical with the deaths of individual human beings". Moral questions are not resolved by majority decision. But the small appeal of the negative argument suggests that it goes against strong moral intuitions, and this, combined with the absence of solid evidence in its support, give the positive argument some clout. At least, we cannot say that people are clearly wrong to defend sovereignty by means of force. The question of whether or not there is a right of self-defence against political aggression has no conclusive answer in either positive or negative terms. What we have in hand is, in other words, a case of *moral indeterminacy*, and the indeterminacy justification of partiality, as adduced in chapter 3, applies. This says that political leaders have a special responsibility to look after the interests of national citizens when moral considerations do not definitely favour one of the possible solutions to a practical problem. It would therefore be wrong not to mobilize military defence against political aggression. The only thing that might reverse this conclusion is a clear popular votum to the contrary, as people can always direct their government to act against national interests.

4 The costs of war

It is one thing to say that a state has a right to defend itself against aggression, whether lethal or political, and another thing to say that political leaders are always justified in exercising this right. The last assumption holds true only if the right of self-defence is *absolute*. The defining feature of an absolute right is that it can always be rightfully exercised. Its normative force is strong enough to withstand all countervailing considerations, which is to say that it constitutes a conclusive reason of action. A *defeasible* right, by contrast, is a *pro tanto* consideration that must always be taken it into account but need not always be respected and should not invariably be acted on, as it may be defeated by stronger, countervailing considerations. This section and the next look at two arguments to the effect that countervailing considerations may – and frequently will – outweigh the right of national self-defence.

One such argument says that what is objectionable about military defence of sovereignty is not that it inevitably causes loss of life, but that the death score will be very high. Although the general question of whether or not sovereignty can be defended by lethal means has no definite answer, there is an answer to the question of whether or not such defence is permissible when very many lives will be lost, and the answer is negative. The situation is no longer morally indeterminate. The negative consequences of military resistance are disproportionate to the negative consequences of no resistance; hence, appeasement – giving in to aggression – is the right reaction. To say this, we need not be able to specify with precision the relative values of life and political freedom. The assumption is that a very high number of deaths anyway tips the scale in favour of appeasement. This will be called the *disproportionality argument*. It does not rule out military action as soon as the costs of defence exceed the costs of appeasement, but only when the former are out of proportion to the latter.[24]

The last phrase is, of course, open to many interpretations. How many deaths are "too many" to warrant military self-defence? Some of those who advance the disproportionality argument believe there is no need to answer this question. The toll will always be high enough to say that violence is unwarranted. Appeasement is always preferable from a moral point of view because any reasonable threshold of justified deaths is bound to be exceeded. Erasmus of Rotterdam ([1517] 1964, p. 192) was of this view: "No peace, regardless of the injustice it involves, should be passed over in favor of war. A sober consideration of the results of any war will weigh the scales in favor of peace." This will be called the presumption of disproportionality. Erasmus buttressed it by noting that war will not only cause death, but also wreck material and spiritual values. He asked us to "earnestly consider the moral degeneration and absence of public discipline, whose restoration will be a very tedious matter", and described in detail the economic disasters of war: "Skilled labor, art, and commerce rapidly decay. The banks are closed", and so on (ibid., p. 199). Although morals and money do not call for as much concern as human lives, their inclusion in the picture provides additional reasons to think that the moral costs of defending sovereignty will always be disproportionate to the costs of appeasement.

The disproportionality argument does not only imply that a state will be wrong to fend off political aggression by force. It may be wrong to take this course in the face of lethal aggression, too. It is conceivable that the moral costs of military action will exceed the costs of appeasement even when appeasement is tantamount to sacrificing national lives, not just national freedoms. Thus, the disproportionality argument casts doubt on the legitimacy of national self-defence in general. Indeed, Erasmus (ibid., p. 192) assumes "that the cause is a just one and the end victorious" before he tells us to "carefully weigh the advantages and the disadvantages involved and attentively judge whether the means justify the end".

The disproportionality argument has something to say for it. It can be premised on the *weak consequentialist principle*, put forth in chapter 1. If, in a situation of choice, one alternative brings about considerably better consequences than another, the former should be chosen before the latter. This principle has strong *prima facie* plausibility, but leaves open the question of when the consequences of one action are considerably better than those of another. The disproportionality argument fills in this gap by suggesting one context where the weak consequentialist principle may be relevant. If the loss of human lives or economic prosperity that follows upon military defence is out of proportion to the loss of freedoms or lives that results from appeasement, appeasement is the right course of action.

The disproportionality argument does not, however, translate immediately into a *presumption* of disproportionality. There is no basis for saying that the moral costs of military defence against political or lethal aggression are always out of proportion to the costs of appeasement. The reason is simply that some wars do not cause death and destruction on a very large scale. They are limited in duration and destruction, and their moral rationale is not obviously invalidated by countervailing consequentialist considerations. As far as such wars are concerned, the choice between defence and appeasement is made in a situation of moral indeterminacy, and the indeterminacy justification of national partiality applies. Now, advocates of appeasement may object that there is always a *risk* that a war of self-defence will be too costly. When the crucial decision is to be made, political leaders are largely ignorant of how things will go, and they may well underrate the likelihood of high death rates and great destruction. In general, it may seem that "of all the tests for judging whether to resort to or participate in war, this one balancing an evil or good effect against another is open to the greatest uncertainty" (Ramsey 1968, p. 195). This brings up the problem of risky policy that was discussed in chapter 3. The principle of partiality in decision under ignorance says that a trustee should be more concerned not to jeopardize the interests of his principal than avoiding risks to people who have no special claim on him. This implies that a government that has to decide whether or not military defence will be exceedingly costly in order to find out whether or not consequentialist considerations favour appeasement, must make sure not to err on the side of too little concern about national interests. Both appeasement and resort to force are options that might eventually occasion moral regret, but some regrets – such as those involved in sacrificing legitimate national interests – are worse than others.

What has been said above presupposes that national citizens are always best served if their government put up military defence against external aggression. This is, of course, no foregone conclusion. The death and debasement that ensue from war may fall upon all parties involved, and the disproportionality argument applies regardless of whose lives or society are destroyed as long as what is destroyed is out of proportion to the value of turning back aggression. This calls for a slight amendment of the previous argument. Political leaders who do not know whether moral considerations call for military defence or appeasement, should take the course that is best for national citizens, whether this is resistance or appeasement.

5 Killing the innocent

There is a second line of argument leading to the conclusion that war of self-defence will generally be immoral even if its cause is just. It says that all wars, regardless of purpose, will have to be fought by immoral means.

I have so far talked about resort to force without distinguishing between ways and means of fighting, but distinctions must now be made on this score. In the just war tradition, they are another legacy of medieval Christendom. During the centuries of ecclesiastical hegemony in intellectual life, principles of *jus ad bellum* were supplemented by rules of *jus in bello* which define proper conduct in war. They require political authorities, as well as generals and soldiers, to observe certain restraints on the conduct of hostilities. The general idea is that a just cause is no warrant of unjust behaviour. This echoes the Pauline principle: *facimus mala ut reniant bona* (it is never right to do evil that good may come).

Rules of restraint were first introduced in the form of bans on the use of cruel or inhumane weapons. Thus, the cross bow was prohibited by ecclesiastical decree in the High Middle Ages. Christian theorists also demanded that each constituent part of a military campaign be carried out with the right intention, meaning that the political and personal antagonisms which inescapably arise during conflict must not be allowed to overshadow the love one should always retain for one's enemies. One should fight with a view to making people realize and recant their errors, not for vindictive purposes. (Johnson 1975, pp. 40–41). This idea is closely related to the requirement of moderation in armed conflict. Combatants should take care not to cause unnecessary suffering or wreak excessive damage in the pursuit of their war aims. According to Thomas Aquinas, it is lawful "to repel force by force, provided one does not exceed the limits of a blameless defence" (quoted in Ramsey 1961, p. 40).[25]

For our purpose, the most important rule of *jus in bello* is the principle of *discrimination*. It rests on the assumption that certain people must not be victimized by military action. A state that has a just cause still fights an unjust war if it does not discriminate between legitimate and illegitimate targets of warfare. The first notable statement of this rule is the so-called "Peace of God", a part of thirteenth century Church law, which turns on the status of those who do not participate directly in warfare because they are servants of the Church or engaged in productive and mercantile activities. The underlying idea is that defensive measures should be directed only against people who share in the *responsibility* for aggression. Thus, the citizens of an aggressor state are not collectively responsible for what their government do. A person must be an accomplice in the misdeeds of his country before he can be taken to account and made to pay for them. Citizenship does not suffice to implicate him. Even in a just war of self-defence, one should take care to spare the innocent. This is, of course, only a special application of the harm principle that was set out in chapter 1.

The status of innocence is usually determined on the basis of participation in military activity. Overt actions, not the cast of people's minds, are what matters. Expressions of patriotism do not, for example, imply that a person shares responsibility for the aggressive designs of his state. In practice, guilt and innocence are inferred from functional criteria. When the discrimination principle is translated into operational terms, it refers to "combatants" and "non-combatants", soldiers and civilians, those who have a say in decisions on peace and war and a hand in planning and carrying out military operations, and those who take no part in military activities.

The discrimination principle can be made the basis of a general challenge to the legitimacy of defensive war. The point is that large-scale warfare inevitably takes a heavy toll of civilian lives. There is in practice now way military campaigns can be carried out without killing innocent people. Political and military leaders may do what they can to discriminate between legitimate and illegitimate targets, but their efforts will largely be in vain, as military operations cannot be kept apart from the places where civilians live and work. This may be called the *presumption of indiscriminate warfare*. It implies that the justice of military defence, as judged by considerations of *jus ad bellum*, is cancelled out by its injustice according to the standard of *jus in bello*.

The presumption of indiscriminate warfare need not imply that all wars are equally indiscriminate. It says, rather, that the conduct of war practically always violates the discrimination principle, and that the violations are gross, that is, not just minor transgressions of, but widespread offenses against the protected status of innocent people. This is an empirical claim, but hardly a controversial one. Few wars take place without heavy civilian tolls.[26]

The presumption of indiscriminate warfare implies that it is mostly wrong to exercise the right of national self-defence. It is, in effect, another argument for appeasement, supplementing the disproportionality argument of the previous section. But the latter involves consequentialist considerations about the relative costs of different policies, while the presumption of indiscriminate warfare is based on the deontological assumption that innocent people must not be killed, whatever the consequences. It derives directly from the harm principle.

The discrimination principle is ambiguous on one score. It does not tell whether every action that kills an innocent person is wrong or if this only applies to actions that kill innocent people on purpose. The doctrine of double effect, which comes from Catholic theory, defines the principle narrowly to bar only intentional killing, not killing that occurs as a side-effect – even a foreseen side-effect – of an action whose aim is something else. Thus, if a state sends bombers to destroy military installations in an invading country, and these installations are situated close to civilian housing, many innocents will inevitably be killed, but this does not matter, according to the doctrine of double effect, as long as the victims are not targeted. By contrast, a broad interpretation of the discrimination principle sets no store by the last consideration. It says simply that any action that can be foreseen to kill an innocent person, is wrong. I do not find the doctrine of double effect persuasive. It makes the wrongness of killing innocent people too much a question of what the agents have in mind, and pays too little attention to the victims. Thus, it shifts the focus from what seems most disturbing about such killing – the fact that innocent people die – to problems of comparatively less concern. I shall therefore disregard the doctrine of double effect in the following and start from the broad interpretation of the discrimination principle. The question is if this principle is correct and, if so, if it grounds a presumption to the effect that defensive war is illegitimate.

The discrimination principle has been challenged by both practitioners of foreign policy and political theorists. A notion of collective responsibility, which the principle rejects, has been invoked in the present century to justify highly consequential decisions. Here is President Truman, addressing the American people in defence of the atomic bomb dropped on Hiroshima in 1945: "We have used [the bomb] against those who attacked us without warning at Pearl Harbor, against those who have starved and beaten and executed American prisoners of war, against those who have abandoned all pretence of obeying international laws of warfare" (quoted in Wasserstrom 1971, p. 301). This is to depart conspicuously from the premise that aggressive designs can be ascribed only to people who actually perform acts of aggression. Truman's purpose may have been to placate vindictive American sentiments, but the idea that only direct participants in war are legitimate targets of warfare has also met with philosophical opposition. George Mavrodes (1975, pp. 122–123) argues that the standard interpretation of innocence and guilt is predicated on an inapposite analogy between acts of war and everyday criminal activity. It is a moral axiom that people should be punished only for the crimes they commit. Thus, the criminal's family should not be made to pay for his conduct, however much they support him with a livelihood. A direct involvement in unlawful schemes is a necessary condition of criminal responsibility, but things stand differently with respect to responsibility for acts of war.

> [W]arfare, unlike ordinary criminal activity, is not an activity in which individuals engage qua individuals or as members of voluntary associations. They enter into wars as members of nations. It is more proper to say that the nation is at war than that its soldiers are at war. (ibid., p. 123)

If people enter into warfare not as individuals, but as members of nations, soldiers and civilians occupy equivalent roles, and any treatment permissible with respect to the former is permissible with respect to the latter as well. If so, the right of national self-defence may be exercised without regard to the discrimination principle. However, Mavrodes' argument begs an important question by suggesting that citizens of an aggressive nation cannot choose whether or not to "engage in" the aggressive actions of their government. He assumes that they have an undeniable part in all national activities as members of the nation, while the discrimination principle insists on individual responsibility. The discrimination principle is the most plausible point of view on this score. To prove that a person is culpable for policies he plays no part direct part in carrying out, requires more than metaphorical talk about common nationality, which is all Mavrodes has to offer.

But the choice need not be between a blanket condemnation of entire nations and an acquittal of all save soldiers. Some incline to think of responsibility for aggression as a matter of degree. Thus, Michael Walzer asks if it would have been worse, during World War II, to bomb the cities of occupied France to stop Hitler than it was to bomb German cities for the same purpose. He answers affirmatively because "it does make sense to say that there were a great many more people in German cities responsible, in however diminished a degree, for the evil of Nazism than there were in French cities" (Walzer 1974, p. 102). But Walzer says little about the way a person's relative degree of responsibility is to be determined, suggesting only that civilian Germans who "actively supported the Nazi party" thereby became implicated in its aggressive designs.[27] One may, of course, point to the wide category of civilian professions whose major function in time of war is to support military action in various ways. They comprise not only munitions workers, but also employees in the steel industry that produces materials for weapons, people who supply the military forces with what they need to remain combative or operate means of communication that transport everything from new recruits to foodstuffs to the front, as well as all the people who prepare future combatants for active duty through education and propaganda. Such examples do not, however, amount to a new typology of combatants and non-combatants that can replace the traditional distinction between soldiers and civilians. They rather indicate that distinct categories will be hard to define. If we give up the simple distinction between soldiers and civilians and rather portray involvement in war as a matter of degree, it becomes difficult to draw an exact line between the innocent and the guilty. There are many people whose classification will be more or less arbitrary if innocence and guilt shade into one another.

Michael Dummett takes this to mean that the discrimination principle has no moral rationale. "When the issue is a moral one", he argues (1984, p. 35), "we cannot allow that the line is blurred, that an action may with equal justice be said to be wrong or not to be wrong: and so a doubt whether a line can be drawn calls in question the principle which requires it to be drawn." This is akin to saying that all members of an aggressor state are equally responsible for its aggression, although it leaves open the question of how they should be treated. There are two reasons to reject Dummett's argument. First, uncertainty is ubiquitous in moral matters, and if we were to discard all principles that do not yield determinate guidance, we would soon be without any guidance. Second, there is no way we can avoid problems of uncertainty by concentrating on sorting out the clear-cut cases. The ambiguous ones are equally, or even more, pressing. We must therefore abandon the quest for certainty and make up our minds as carefully as possible on the basis of existing evidence.

Where, then, does existing evidence point when it comes to distinguishing between combatants and non-combatants? John Ford ([1944] 1970, p. 20) holds that the onus of proof is on "those who are innovators" in that they accord guilt to people who fall outside the conventional category of combatants. He suggests that "we start with the view that only armed soldiers are guilty combatants", and that "anyone who wants to increase the number of the guilty, and make unarmed civilians legitimate objects of violent repression, has the duty of proving his position" (ibid.). The problem is that we cannot easily tell whether or not the innovators have proved their point. There is some basis for denying that all civilian members of an aggressor state are innocent people whose killing in a defensive war would violate the harm principle, but there is also a basis for deeming them all innocent and saying that military defence is illegitimate whenever it takes a toll of civilian lives, as it usually does.

Let us grant that many civilians are innocents. Does this imply that war of self-defence is illegitimate, despite its just cause, because it inescapably violates the discrimination principle? An imaginary but by no means unrealistic case may help us fix our intuitions. It amounts to a simile of modern warfare which puts the question of how innocent lives should be balanced against primary national interests in a nutshell. I borrow the case from Judith Jarvis Thomson, who calls it *Strategic Bomber*.

> [T]he villainous Bads have invaded noble country Good, and a Good pilot has been ordered to bomb a munitions factory in Bad. Unfortunately, the factory is so situated that if the pilot bombs the factory, some nearby Bad civilians will be killed – let us imagine them to be children, in a nearby children's hospital. Doesn't morality permit the pilot to proceed all the same? But the children are mere bystanders. (Thomson 1991, p. 292)

The last two sentences indicate – and further comments confirm – that Thomson is unsure of how this case should be assessed. Resorting to a simpler analogue of Strategic Bomber, she advances the following argument: A person who can only avoid being run over by a trolley by firing an antitank gun at it, has no right to do so if he will thereby blow up not only the trolley, but also a bystander who happens to stand near its track. The duty not to kill an innocent person is, in other words, seen as a weightier consideration than the safety of the person whom the trolley will kill. Strategic Bomber is different in that the "pilot's proceeding … is part of a larger process in which the noble Goods are defending themselves in a war being waged against them by the villainous Bads", and this fact makes "it the case that the (long-range) stakes are higher than we have been told in being told about those children in the hospital next door to the munitions factory" (ibid., p. 297). In view of this, Thomson concludes, it is permissible for the pilot to proceed.

Thomson's argument begs a question that is central for our purpose: are the stakes of national self-defence high enough to permit defensive measures that will kill innocent people? This question hardly has a determinate answer, however. Thomson admits having "to bypass as too hard the question how the fact of war affects questions about self-defence" (ibid., p. 298), which seems the only reasonable course. Moral indeterminacy inheres in the choice whether or not to fight aggression by military means.

For the government of an invaded country, the indeterminate situation amounts to a tragic dilemma. Whatever choice it makes, it does something wrong. This goes for killing innocent people, like children in a hospital near a munitions factory, no less than giving up political sovereignty to an invading state that will deprive national citizens of their freedoms and possibly imprison, torture and execute some of them. Political authorities cannot avoid moral regret, but, as stated before, some regrets are worse than others. As a trustee of national citizens, the government is obligated to place national safety before countervailing considerations when there is no determinate answer to the question of which is weightiest. Hence, it should exercise its right of national self-defence even if it can only do so by violating the discrimination principle and, hence, the harm principle.

6 Conclusion

This chapter confirms what most people believe: a state has a right to defend itself against lethal as well as political aggression by means of force. But the argument also shows that the justification of this common belief raises many vexed questions. I have looked at two suggestive arguments for appeasement – the disproportionality argument which involves consequentialist considerations about the relative costs of different policies, and the presumption of indiscriminate warfare which derives from the deontological assumption that innocent people must not be killed whatever the consequences. Neither argument is strong enough to overturn the right of national self-defence; nor, however, do considerations of self-defence obviously override consequentialist and deontological reasons of appeasement. These considerations, rather, win out because a government must take particular care not to err on the side of insufficient concern about national interests. The two principles of legitimate partiality that were invoked in chapter 3 play a crucial role in justifying the right of national self-defence.

6 War of Defence: Moral Principles and Legal Rules

1 Introduction

The rationale of a moral right of national self-defence was established in chapter 5. Should there be a *legal* right of national defence as well? Section 2 will show that such a right is incorporated in contemporary international law. Pragmatic concerns may, however, call for its abolition. An argument to this effect will be discussed and rejected in section 3. Then I ask what form the legal right of self-defence ought to take. Should military action be permitted only in case a state is under attack, or even for the purpose of forestalling or deterring attack? This question will be explored in sections 4 and 5.

2 National self-defence in contemporary law

In this century, the legal debate about armed conflict has largely revolved around three documents. The first is the *Covenant of the League of Nations*, adopted in 1919. Its emphasis is on peaceful resolution of impending military crises. It says that governments should submit their disputes to arbitration or inquiry by the Council of the League, which then recommends a settlement (articles XII, XIII and XV). If a member of the League goes to war before such measures have been tried, "it shall *ipso facto* be deemed to have committed an act of war against all other Members of the League" and will be liable to various forms of sanction (article XVI). It might seem that the Covenant permits resort to force regardless of cause provided all obligatory precautions have been taken. However, article X alludes to a principle of *jus ad bellum* that has later become the crux of 20th century law: "Members of the League undertake to respect and preserve as against external aggression the territorial integrity and existing political independence of all Members of the League". This is tantamount to a ban on the use of force for all purposes save in national self-defence.

The next major piece of international legislation grew out of efforts in the 1920s to obtain American guarantees of French security in relation to Germany. The United States responded by proposing a universal declaration on the renunciation of war. This declaration, which became known as the *Kellogg–Briand Pact*, was adopted in 1928 and eventually became signed by more than sixty states. It contains a blanket proscription of military action under all circumstances. Article II reads that "the settlement or solution of all disputes or conflicts of whatever nature or of whatever origin they may be, … shall never be sought except by pacific means". No distinction is drawn between just and unjust causes of war; war is outlawed regardless of purpose. An air of unreality surrounded the Kellogg–Briand Pact from the start, and exceptions were immediately taken to its uncompromising principles. The United States' Secretary of State said that "every nation is free at all times to defend its territory from attack or invasion and it alone is competent to decide whether circumstances require recourse to war in self-defense"; hence, the Pact left intact the "inherent right of self-defense" (quoted in Johnson 1973, p. 467). This qualification, conjoined with the League of Nations' prohibition of aggression, give the main outlines of the two-pronged legal doctrine that was to emerge after World War II. It says that a state (i) must never violate the territorial integrity or political sovereignty of another state, but (ii) can defend itself by means of force against armed attack.

The all-important source of international law on armed conflict after 1945 is the *United Nations Charter*. Among the "Purposes of the United Nations", listed in article 1(1), the first is to "maintain international peace and security". Two corollaries of this objective are stated in articles 2(3) and 2(4):

> *Article 2(3):* All Members [of the United Nations] shall settle their international disputes by peaceful means in such a manner that international peace and security, and justice, are not endangered.
>
> *Article 2(4):* All members shall refrain in their international relations from the threat or use of force against the territorial integrity or political independence of any state, or in any other manner inconsistent with the Purposes of the United Nations.

These articles raise several questions of interpretation. First, it is not clear what one should make of the inclusion in article 2(3) of "justice" as an objective of peaceful settlement alongside "peace and security". It may imply that threats to security and breaches of peace are the only injustices, but if so, the phrase is redundant. Or injustice may be something else, so that the inclusion of "justice" qualifies the ban on force, implying that forceful settlement of conflict is prohibited if it endangers peace and security *as well as* justice, but not if it vindicates justice. The latter interpretation is, however, inconsistent with article 2(4), and it appears that the reference to justice is really a redundancy.

Second, what is meant by the last phrase of article 2(4) – "in any other manner inconsistent with the Purposes of the United Nations"? As pointed out, the foremost purpose of the United Nations is to "maintain international peace and security", and "any other manner" may simply be read as all threats or uses of force that jeopardize peace and security without being directed at the territorial integrity or political independence of any state. The distinction between direct and indirect use of force, elaborated by Hilaire McCoubrey and Nigel D. White (1992, p. 32), seems germane at this point. By direct use, they intend involvements in regular inter-state war, while indirect use consists in providing one party in an intra-state war with money, arms or troops. The latter does not obviously amount to encroachments on integrity or independence, but is "inconsistent with the Purposes of the United Nations".

Articles 2(3) and 2(4) constitute the first part of the two-pronged doctrine of just war that is embodied in contemporary international law. The second part finds expression in articles 39, 42, 51 and 53. It involves two major exceptions to the ban on using force in international relations. In the first place, article 42 says that the Security Council can authorize the use of military force by members of the United Nations. So it may, says article 39, after having determined the existence of a "threat to the peace, breach of the peace, or act of aggression". As measures "to maintain or restore international peace and security", article 42 lists "demonstrations, blockade, and other operations by air, sea, or land forces". Moreover, article 53 states that the Security Council can also extend its authorization of military action to regional organizations. Briefly put, articles 39, 42 and 53 allow concerted military action directed at states that violate articles 2(3) and 2(4).

In the second place, article 51 asserts that states may resort to force, individually or collectively, in response to attack: "Nothing in the present Charter shall impair the inherent right of individual or collective self-defense if an armed attack occurs against a Member of the United Nations." There are two conditions on this exception to articles 2(3) and 2(4): acts of self-defence "shall be immediately reported to the Security Council", and they shall cease when "the Security Council has taken measures necessary to maintain international peace and security". The last condition has greatest interest, but it makes no heavy inroads into the right of self-defence. McCoubrey and White (1992, p. 102) interpret article 51 "to mean that only those measures which can effectively take the place of potential actions in self-defence can be said to *suspend* the right. If the measures prove ineffective, then the right of self-defence must revive".

Article 51 does not permit the use of force in response to every breach of 2(3) and 2(4) – only in response to armed attack. This implies that use of force which falls short of armed attack – e.g., indirect use or isolated border incidents – does not warrant military self-defence. The right of self-defence is, in other words, a more limited exception to articles 2(3) and 2(4) than that contained in articles 39, 42 and 53. While the Security Council can authorize military measures in reaction to indirect use of force in so far as it constitutes "threat to the peace", states cannot adopt such measures on their own initiative. Moreover, article 51 does not, on the face of it, legalize acts of self-defence in response to *threats* of force. The phrase "armed attack" suggests ongoing military operations, not mere preparations. We will, however, return to some problems with this limitation in section 4.

The prohibition on using force without authorization by the Security Council or in self-defence against armed attack, has become *jus cogens* or peremptory law in relations among states. This is to say that no state can exempt itself from it (Cassese 1986, p. 26). But is this the way international law of armed conflict ought to be? A negative answer can take three forms. First, one might argue that all uses of force, including war of self-defence, is illegitimate and ought to be outlawed. This is the pacifist position, which was rejected in chapter 5. Second, it may be held that war of defence should be prohibited and the use of force for other purposes permitted, but I do not believe this view has many adherents. If the right of national self-defence is to be abolished from international law it must be because no rule of *jus ad bellum* belongs there at all. This suggests a third argument: the law should not distinguish between just and unjust war, but delete all rules of *jus ad bellum*. This cannot be a moral argument, as moral concerns support a right of self-defence, but the abolition of *jus ad bellum* might be grounded in pragmatic considerations, and the next section will examine an attempt to this effect.

3 Vattel's argument

The idea that international law should abolish all distinctions between just and unjust objectives of war can be traced to Emmerich de Vattel, the most influential legal theorist of the seventeenth century. The separation of moral and legal questions is a leitmotif of his major work, *Le Droit des Gens*. It makes clear that jurisprudence is not a question of rewriting moral principles in another language. While the principles of natural law are, in the last analysis, decisive even in legal matters, there is no simple one-to-one correspondence between these principles and the practical provisions of international law.

Vattel distinguishes between two perspectives on the rights and wrongs of foreign policy. The *internal* perspective belongs to the statesman who faces a morally charged decision and consults his conscience to find out what the law of nature demands. Such consultation is incumbent on governments,[28] and the internal point of view discloses a law of nations that is "everywhere and at all points the same as the natural law", reflecting the "inner law" that is enshrined in the individual statesman's "voice of conscience" (Vattel [1758] 1970, vol. III, p. 113). The natural law contains, in particular, principles of just war, and these leave only room for defensive use of force. "A nation must", Vattel says, "have received an injury, or be clearly threatened with one before it is authorized to take up arms as having a just ground for war" (ibid., p. 113).

How do we get from the inner law of conscience to the public law of nations? Vattel holds that "the just and reasonable application of a rule requires that the application be made in a manner suited to the nature of the subject", and "we must not conclude that the Law of Nations is everywhere and at all points the same as the natural law, except for a difference of subjects, so that no other change need be made than to substitute Nations for individuals" (ibid., p. 104). This introduces the *external* perspective on political morality. We need a basis for accommodating and arbitrating between contending claims and conflicting policies, and a direct appeal to natural law, as revealed by the inner law of conscience, will not do. We cannot, in particular, adjudicate an armed conflict by reference to the principle that "[h]e alone whose sword is drawn from necessity and in the cause of justice has the right to make war" (ibid., p. 121). It would be of no avail because of the institutional weaknesses of the international legal order. When moral principles of *jus ad bellum* are translated into legal provisions, modifications must be made to attune them to the circumstances of the international anarchy. Vattel is, indeed, led to a most radical conclusion: The distinction between just and unjust causes of war has no place at all in international law. Pragmatic considerations suggest that "regular war … must be accounted just on both sides" (ibid., p. 123; italics deleted).

The reason is two-fold. First, Vattel alludes to the irrelevance argument whose general form was outlined in chapter 4. In defence of accounting war "just on both sides", he says that "any other rule would be impracticable as between Nation and Nation, since they recognize no common judge". There is no superior authority that can tell just from unjust causes and enforce legal pronouncements.

> [H]ow shall this law be made to prevail in the quarrels of the Nations and sovereigns who live together in the state of nature? They recognize no superior who shall decide between them and define the rights and obligations of each, who shall say to this one: 'You have a right to take up arms, to attack your enemy and subdue him by force', and to that other: 'Your hostilities are unwarranted, your victories are but murder, your conquests are but the spoil of robbery and pillage'. (ibid.)

Second, there is a risk that legal rules of just war will be counterproductive. Vattel believes, more specifically, that they would contribute to worsening the horrors of war, allowing certain states to fight under the banner of righteousness and thereby injecting their conduct with an extra zeal that makes it all the more difficult to restrain warfare through rules of *jus in bello*. This corresponds to the counterfinality argument of chapter 4. It lies at the core of Vattel's case against a legal right of national self-defence. Restraints on warfare are uppermost in his mind. He proposes the elimination of *jus ad bellum* as a legal category in order to reinforce rules of *jus in bello*. To grant a government a right cause and brand its adversary as an outlaw is a recipe for unrestrained warfare. As there is no superior authority to distinguish between true and false pretensions of righteousness, all belligerents may plead justice and act as if they have the law on their side.

> [S]ince each Nation claims to have justice on its side, it will arrogate to itself all the rights of war and claim that its enemy has none, that his hostilities are but deeds of robbery, acts in violation of the Law of Nations, and deserving of punishment by all Nations. The decision of the rights at issue will not be advanced thereby, and the contest will become more cruel, more disastrous in its effects, and more difficult of termination. (ibid., pp. 121–122)

Vattel does not, to be sure, relinquish the distinction between just and unjust war altogether. According to natural law, force is a legitimate resort only in self-defence. If a national leader goes to war on other purposes, he acts immorally and will have to answer before his conscience. The public law of nations must, however, remain silent on this score in order not to "increase the evils of human society while seeking to prevent them" (ibid., p. 124). Law is "established from necessity and for the avoidance of greater evils. It does not confer upon him whose cause is unjust any true rights capable of justifying his conduct and appeasing his conscience, but merely makes his conduct legal in the sight of men, and exempt him from punishment" (ibid.; italics deleted).

This is Vattel's pragmatic argument for the abandonment of *jus ad bellum* from international law. It casts doubt on the practical possibility of combining legal warrants of war with normative restraints on warfare. Such doubt arose, Inis Claude (1980, p. 90) says, when "the medieval plausibility of the application of the just war idea gave way to its modern improbability". The moral and political consensus of European Christendom was replaced by the quarrels of self-willed, sovereign rulers in a "system not equipped to make the difficult distinctions required by just war theory". Owing to the risk that a legal distinction between just and unjust causes would aggravate rather than reduce international violence, there were tactical reasons to place all adversaries on a par and concentrate on regulating their conduct during hostilities.

Vattel's argument for the abandonment of *jus ad bellum* is reflected in positive international law of the eighteenth and nineteenth centuries. Up to 1914, governments had an unrestricted legal right to take up arms, which was affirmed in article 2 of the Hague Convention for the Pacific Settlement of International Disputes, adopted in 1907. Prior to World War I, the law of war was extremely generous (Cassese 1986, p. 24).[29]

Vattel's argument implies that contemporary international law ought to be revised to eliminate the warrant of defensive war. Is the argument valid? Its evaluation can be seen as a problem of balancing two risks. On the one hand, there is a risk that retaining the legal warrant of national self-defence contributes to making warfare less restrained and more destructive than it would otherwise have been. On the other hand, there is also a risk that abandoning all rules of *jus ad bellum* would result in more frequent wars between states. Vattel diminishes the latter risk by suggesting that a ban on all but defensive wars is ineffective owing to the institutional weaknesses of the international legal order. There is, in other words, no chance that the world will become more violent than it already is if every war is accounted just on both sides. Legal distinctions between just and unjust objectives make no practical difference, and only the retainment of legal rules of *jus ad bellum* involves a real risk. If we are to believe Vattel, pragmatic considerations provide an open and shut case for eliminating the right of national self-defence from contemporary law.

His argument suffers, however, from both empirical and logical shortcomings. There is, in the first place, no basis for discounting altogether the practical import of legal distinctions between just and unjust causes of war. Even prior to World War I, when international law permitted states to go to war for any purpose, governments did not normally consider themselves absolved from justifying military action in terms of just causes. They were reluctant to avail themselves of their legal prerogative and usually adhered to traditional warrants of war, notably national self-defence (Claude Jr. 1980, p. 89; Elbe 1939, pp. 685–687).

In the second place, the risk that wars will become more frequent if their causes are accounted just on both sides can hardly be discounted without at the same discounting the risk that warfare will be more destructive if only one party can claim to have the law on its side. Doubts about the effectiveness of legal rules of *jus ad bellum* entail doubts about the effectiveness of rules of *jus in bello*. The role of the former in preventing war cannot be diminished without simultaneously diminishing the role of the latter in restraining war. Hence, if there is no risk involved in abandoning the right of national self-defence, there is no risk involved in retaining it. One of Vattel's pivotal premises tends to undercut the other, and his argument can only be saved by recasting it. One may argue that the risk that wars become more frequent if international law no longer distinguishes just from unjust causes of war is *less* than the risk that warfare becomes more destructive if this distinction is made. Then we will be comparing two genuine risks. The recast argument cannot, however, be grounded in general observations about the institutional weaknesses of the international legal order. Such weaknesses hardly hurt the effectiveness of international law more with respect to rules of *jus ad bellum* than in the case of rules of *jus in bello*. The comparison of risks in terms of relative magnitude must be premised on detailed arguments about the likelihoods of different courses of events. Vattel offers nothing to this effect. His argument fails, on both logical and empirical grounds, to prove that international law should abolish all distinctions between just and unjust causes of war. The legal right of self-defence withstands his challenge.

4 Self-defence and anticipation

It was pointed out in section 3 that the United Nations Charter lays down a limited right of national self-defence. Article 51 permits military action only in response to armed attack. I shall now look closer at the most controversial aspect of this limitation – the notion that only use of force, not threat of force, warrants self-defence.

At issue is war of *anticipation*. Must a state wait until an attack is on the way before it resorts to force in defence, or is it allowed to take anticipatory action? A war of anticipation is an attack that is launched in order to forestall an impending attack. Technically speaking, a state that anticipates wages an offensive war. If, however, its objective is purely defensive, we may call it a war of defence in an extended sense – extended to take account of the fact that it is sometimes impossible to put up effective defence if military action has to be deferred until an attack is on the way. I shall first go into some problems of legal interpretation and then ask what international law ought to say about self-defence by anticipation.

The letter of the law is, as we have seen, plain. Article 51 permits military action only "if an armed attack occurs". Thus, the right of national self-defence comes into force only after a state has suffered an attack. But the literal reading of the UN Charter is not obviously faithful to the spirit of the law. It may be too restrictive. To be sure, most international lawyers see no problem on this score. They countenance resort to force only when an armed attack has been mounted and is on the way, confining the legal right of national self-defence to what I shall call *pure* self-defence. Now, the only difference between pure self-defence and anticipatory self-defence is that the defender strikes first in the latter case. Some lawyers hold that, if we go by the spirit of international law, first strike is sometimes warranted, and the letter of the law should be revised accordingly. This may be called the *revisionist* thesis. It implies that the existence of an overt military threat may justify a state in striking out against an impending attack before it materializes.

An outspoken proponent of the revisionist thesis is Myres McDougal, whose view is summed up succinctly here:

> According to Professor Myres McDougal, Article 51 cannot be taken to read that a military response in self-defense is permitted if, and only if, an armed attack has actually occurred. I would be against reason and nature, particularly in the age of jets, rockets and nuclear weapons, to interpret Article 51 so literally as to preclude a victim from using force in self-defence until it has actually been attacked. From this he goes on to say that a state may use military force when it "regards itself as intolerably threatened by the activities of another". If customary international law, the doctrine of necessity, and human reason have always permitted pre-emptive strikes against an anticipated rather than only an actual attack, it follows in McDougal's argument that no nation can have intended, by the adherence to Article 51, to bound itself to sit still while another nation prepares to strike a first, and possibly lethal, blow. (Franck 1970, p. 821)

There is, of course, room for doubt about the true nature of many anticipatory actions. Intentions may be feigned, fears exaggerated and defensive objectives inflated. For the moment, however, these practical problems will be bracketed. The question is if a state may take military action to seize the initiative from an adversary that shows every sign of preparing for attack. McDougal advances two arguments to ground an affirmative answer. He states that the strict conception of self-defence is (a) against "reason" and "nature" and (b) contrary to customary law and unlikely to be intended by states adhering to the United Nations Charter. Proposition (a) suggests that the literal reading of the Charter, which limits legitimate defence to military action against an ongoing attack, must be set aside on moral grounds, although no specification of these grounds are offered. I shall defer the discussion of this point and concentrate first on proposition (b). It may be factorized into three assertions: (i) states have customarily asserted and acknowledged a right of anticipatory self-defence; (ii) customary law is the proper basis for interpreting the UN Charter; hence (iii) the literal interpretation of the Charter is untenable.

Assertion (i) has much to be said for it. Prior to the adoption of the UN Charter, it was widely held that international law permitted anticipatory self-defence whenever a government believed it was about to be attacked. It is even arguable that a right of preventive war was generally recognized before 1945. There are, to be sure, serious reservations on both scores (Brownlie 1968, pp. 251ff.), but let us, for the sake of the argument, assume that the right of anticipation was part of customary law before 1945. What, then, about assertion (ii) – the claim that customary law should guide interpretation of the UN Charter? There is a simple, but potentially devastating, objection to it. A prime purpose of the UN Charter was to overturn previous principles of just war. Thus, the notion that force may be used only in response to an actual attack is a deliberate legislative innovation. Rather than revising it by reference to custom, we should realize that it was meant to replace customary law. Cassese (1986, p. 230) says that the "text and drafting history of Article 51 make it abundantly clear that the provision did not intend to leave the pre-existing right of anticipatory self-defence, if any, unaffected". In the same vein, Douglas Lackey (1984, p. 23) professes "little doubt that the intent of Article 51 is to rule out anticipatory self-defense: nations must *wait* until suffering an armed attack before legitimately using unilateral force".

But the revisionist thesis does not only say that the literal reading of the UN Charter runs contrary to customary law; it also asserts that the strict conception of self-defence is against "reason" and "nature". This is to say that there are moral reasons to incorporate the option of anticipation in the right of national self-defence, and to suggest that the letter of the law be revised accordingly. The most straightforward way of buttressing such a suggestion draws on considerations of military expediency. Basically, the argument is that anticipation is permissible in so far as it is a necessary condition of successful national self-defence. To take the initiative in an impending military struggle sometimes provides considerable strategic advantage, owing to technological and logistic factors. "Attack is the best defence" was the slogan of General von Schlieffen, the main German authority on military strategy prior to World War I, and although the Schlieffen Plan may reflect a misguided "cult of the offensive" (Evera 1986, pp. 83–84), the underlying thesis is often a sound diagnosis of constraints and opportunities on the battlefield. Taking the initiative enables a state to choose the time, location and mode of fighting.

> Airplanes cannot stay aloft indefinitely. We might thus be under strong pressure to strike before the enemy air force gets into the air and before we must again land to refuel. Populations cannot be totally mobilized indefinitely, if the civilian economy is to continue to function. We might thus again strike while our army is mobilized, and while the enemy's battalions are not, to avoid his waiting to strike when we again have had to be demobilized to return to civilian occupations. (Quester 1977, p. 4)

If states have a right of self-defence, why should they not be permitted to anticipate so as to make sure that defensive efforts are in fact effective? Julius Stone (1958, pp. 98 and 100; italics deleted) speaks of the "absurdities" of the view that, "at a pinch", when all non-violent means of aborting an attack is exhausted, a state "is bound by law to wait for its own destruction". It can hardly be *illegitimate* for a state to strike first in order to pre-empt an imminent attack if its defensive forces will otherwise be put at considerable disadvantage. But is there a convincing case for revising international law? Should the legal right of national self-defence be explicitly extended to encompass anticipatory self-defence? At this point, pragmatic considerations enter into the picture. The step from considerations of legitimacy to proposals for legislation cannot be taken without asking what overall effects a legal reform is likely to have. It is arguable that we run a high risk by translating the moral rationale of anticipation into a legal permission. So, at any rate, the *slippery slope* argument of chapter 3 may suggest. Remember its three postulates: (1) If X is permitted, Y will be hard to avoid; (2) Y is morally unacceptable or otherwise undesirable; therefore (3) X must not be permitted. The slippery slope argument against a right of anticipation can be stated as follows: (1) If international law permits war of anticipation, an increasing frequency of *preventive* war will be hard to avoid; (2) an increasing frequency of preventive war is undesirable; hence (3) war of anticipation must not be permitted.

Before I look closer at this argument, the concept of preventive war must be clarified. Bernard Brodie (1959, p. 227) defines military prevention as "a premeditated attack by one country against another, which is unprovoked in the sense that it does not wait upon a specific aggression or other overt action by the target state, and in which the chief and most immediate objective is the destruction of the latter's over-all military power" – or, one may add, significant parts of this power. Unlike anticipation, military prevention does not take place after an immediate risk of armed attack has been apprehended. It is rather a question of weakening an adversary so as to prevent future attack. A case in point is Israel's bombing of a nuclear reactor in Iraq in 1981. It was intended to prevent Iraq from developing nuclear forces that eventually might have become a threat to Israel. By contrast, the Israeli attack on Egypt in 1967 was launched in the midst of conspicuous Egyptian preparations for war. It had, at least initially, every appearance of being a war of anticipation.

Proposition (1) of the slippery slope argument says that the legalization of anticipation will lead to a higher frequency of preventive war. To ground this assumption, two premises will be needed: (i) Legal permission of anticipation will inevitably generate more permissive attitudes to preventive war, and (ii) more permissive attitudes will lead to more frequent resort to such war. The evaluation of proposition (1) may conveniently start with premise (ii). A change of attitude towards greater tolerance of preventive war will remove an important restraint against it only if such war often presents itself to states as strategically advantageous. Does it? Some analysts think so on the grounds that states appear obsessed by fear and ever ready to augment their margin of safety by striking out at potential enemies. Thus, the Abbé Galiani thought that "foresight" was the actual cause of many a war. "Because one foresees that the House of Hapsburg will increase, because the French, a hundred years from now, will do such a thing, we begin to cut one another's throats right now" (quoted from Schweller 1992, p. 236). Others, however, take a more complacent view. Arnold Wolfers (1962, p. 153) argues that "[e]fforts of security are bound to be experienced as a burden", and "nations will be inclined to minimize these efforts, keeping them at the lowest level that will provide them with what they consider adequate protection". These assumptions point in diametrically opposed directions, and we have no solid evidence for saying where the truth lies (Malnes 1993, ch. 3). Strategic incentives of preventive war cannot, therefore, be counted out. The risk exists that states will often act on such incentives if they can do so with impunity.

Another question that arises in relation to premise (ii) is if more permissive attitudes towards preventive war will significantly affect its frequency. This question cannot, of course, be answered conclusively. We have no way of knowing for sure whether or not the emergence of a more indulgent view of preventive war will make its occurrence more likely, but in so far as attitudes matter at all, greater indulgence makes for a higher likelihood.

Premise (i) of proposition (1) says that a legal permission of anticipation will inevitably generate more permissive attitudes to preventive war. It is arguable that preventive war has so much in common with anticipatory attack that legalization of the latter confers acceptability on the former as well. To be sure, advocates of the revisionist thesis presuppose that a distinction can be made on this score. Thus, William O'Brien (1991, p. 60; italics added) "supports the legal permissibility of preemptive attack in cases where there is a *clear and present* danger of attack, as in the case of Israel's preemptive first strike against Egypt in the 1967 June War". Premise (i) implies, however, that clear and present dangers shade into less clear and more distant ones. Anticipatory and preventive war will have to be distinguished by the temporal proximity of military threats, which is sometimes unproblematic – thus, attacking another state "right now" in order not to become its victim "a hundred years from now" cannot be grouped with military anticipation – but often problematic. No clear line can be drawn between threats that are either too distant or near enough for us to say that actions taken against them constitute military anticipation. If, therefore, military anticipation is legalized, war of prevention will appear in a more favourable light.

This argument does not disprove that military strikes against imminent threats can generally be distinguished from the use of force for preventive purposes. Hence, premise (ii) of proposition (1) is not established beyond reasonable doubt. Neither, however, can it be set aside. Like premise (i), premise (ii) has enough plausibility to confer some credibility on the first part of the slippery slope argument.[30]

The next step of the argument is proposition (2), which says that it would be undesirable if preventive war was to become more frequent. This leads directly to proposition (3) – the conclusion that anticipatory war should be strictly prohibited in order to avoid our landing on the slippery slope. If, therefore, proposition (2) is wrong, the slippery slope argument collapses. Some will shrug at the last suggestion and take the underlying question to be undue, arguing that wars are always unfortunate events and an increase in their frequency always a cause of concern. I have, however, established the legitimacy of war of self-defence and there is no saying that other types of war cannot be legitimate, too.

Thus, before proposition (2) can be assessed, we have to find out if military prevention is legitimate or illegitimate.

Preventive war was defined above as a premeditated military attack that is unprovoked and does not respond to an overt threat of armed attack. It aims at destroying or weakening a state's over-all military power. No one, as far as I know, has proposed the legalization of preventive war, but Emmerich de Vattel saw no difficulty in producing a moral rationale of it. In his view, it was no less legitimate than war of self-defence.

> [W]e know only too well from sad and frequent experience that predominant States rarely fail to trouble their neighbours, to oppress them, and even to subjugate them completely, when they have an opportunity of doing so with impunity. ... Must we await the danger? Must we let the storm gather strength when it might be scattered at its rising? Must we suffer a neighbouring state to grow in power and wait quietly until it is ready to enslave us? Will it be time to defend ourselves when we are no longer able to? (Vattel [1758] 1970, pp. 113–114)

Vattel's rhetorical questions are clearly meant to suggest that there is no reason why preventive war should be condemned if defensive war is condoned. He suggests, in effect, that there is a continuity between the two forms of military action as far as moral rationale is concerned. If we have a right to fight for national freedom by means of force, we must be permitted to do so before our enslavement is a foregone conclusion. Thus, the justification of preventive war need not involve new arguments about the legitimacy of military action. It only adds instrumental considerations of military expediency to what has already been said about the right of national self-defence and the moral permissibility of anticipatory attack. Prevention is countenanced in so far as deferring defensive measures would render effective defence impracticable.

This line of argument has some appeal. It was invoked by political and military leaders in the United States during the late 1940s and early 1950s, when the Soviet Union was about to acquire a large arsenal of nuclear weapons. Suggestions were made that the US should pursue an active policy to prevent this. On one occasion, a secretary of the navy envisaged Americans as the world's first "aggressors for peace"; on another occasion, a commanding officer of the Air War College proposed the use of strategic airpower to "break up Russia's five A-bomb nests" and thus save "civilization" (quoted in Trachtenberg 1988/89, pp. 10 and 20). The moral justification of preventive war was elaborated by

James Burnham in his book of 1947, *Struggle for the World* (quoted in Buhite and Hamel 1990, p. 375):

> If there is good reason to believe that a sudden massive armed blow would ... as compared with waiting for such a blow from the enemy, save many lives and goods, result in less destruction and social disintegration, give a better chance for building a workable world polity, then to strike such a blow, far from being morally wrong, is morally obligatory. If there is to be war in any case, it is hard to comprehend why a war is morally better because it is more difficult, more cruel and costly and bloody.

This argument may be evaluated in two ways. If we attend only to what it says, it seems unassailable. Clearly, if there *is* to be war in any case, it had better be a war of the least bloody and destructive kind. Yet, long-term predictions of peace and war are exceedingly uncertain, and comparisons between possible wars in terms of destructiveness no less so. Burnham's argument leaves considerable room for subjective judgment. One may contend, however, that this reflects a general problem of foreign policy which was noted in chapter 3. Political authorities are always in danger of erring in their beliefs about the prerequisites of national security, and they should always take particular care not to err on the side of excessive optimism. As trustees of national citizens, they must not run a high risk of exposing the nation to aggression – or so, at any rate, the principle of partiality in decision under ignorance says.

On the face of it, this principle implies that a government is permitted (and obligated) to launch a preventive war if national interests would otherwise be put at great risk. It says that political authorities should always do what they believe to be safest in the light of what they know about the consequences of alternative policies at the time of decision. In the present case, however, more than the ubiquitous uncertainty of international relations comes into the picture. The principle that underlies Burnham's argument in favour of preventive war is inherently prone to be misused. Not only will it have to be supplemented with potentially controversial empirical premises before practical conclusions can be elicited from it. That goes for most moral principles. An additional problem is the total absence of precise criteria for assessing the relevant premises. The principle has, so to speak, no built-in conceptual precaution against gross misuse. Burnham says, for example, that a preventive war may be justified if "there is to be war in any case", but in a situation charged by severe conflict and suspicion, this is anybody's guess.

This objection recalls the *vagueness* argument of chapter 4. One is reminded of David Hume's objection to the idea that material resources ought to be distributed with a view to ensuring that possessions are proportional to moral merit. In Hume's view, if "mankind [were] to execute such a law; so great is the uncertainty of merit, both from its natural obscurity, and from the self-conceit of each individual, that no determinate rule of conduct would ever result from it; and the total dissolution of society must be the immediate consequence" (Hume [1777] 1975, p. 193). Similar reservations may be raised about Burnham's argument. The uncertainty surrounding his moral rationale of preventive war is so great, owing to both the natural obscurity of conflict processes and the self-conceit of adversaries, that no determinate rule of foreign policy would ever follow from it. The absence of a discernible boundary between justified and unjustified acts of prevention tells against a general approval of preventive war. It implies that the opportunities for troubling neighbours may become legion if a permissive attitude to such war is allowed to arise and spread.

This sets the stage for a last look at the question of whether or not international law ought to sanction anticipatory self-defence. If such defence is indistinguishable from preventive action, there is a risk that legalizing anticipation will lead, by way of a slippery slope, to permissive attitudes towards the wide and variegated category of preventive war. Legitimate anticipatory self-defence will shade into illegitimate war of prevention, and a legal permission of the former may be used as a cloak of the latter. Here lies a good pragmatic reason not to legalize anticipation in the first place.

Still, a government may find itself incapable of putting up an effective defence if it does not destroy or weaken another state's military power through a premeditated attack, and granted that political authorities should often place considerations of national security above all other concerns, the moral legitimacy of military prevention cannot be ruled out as a matter of principle. This sounds paradoxical. After cautioning against the adoption of a legal rule that risks becoming a cloak of unjust preventive war, I now deny that prevention is always morally wrong, which is to recommend the adoption of a legal rule whose violation is at the same time acknowledged to be morally justified under certain circumstances. The paradox may be resolved as follows. The legal rule that permits only pure defence is recommended because it will have positive effects on positive morality – "the morality actually accepted and shared by a given social group" (Hart 1986, p. 20). The fact that its adoption entails legal condemnation of some legitimate actions is a price one has to pay for these effects. Justified anticipation will have to be judged illegal in order to prevent positive morality from being infected by permissive attitudes towards preventive war. The morally correct principle of national self-defence is not one we ought to incorporate in international law. Indeed, if the law were to mirror morality in every respect, it would have to permit even preventive measures that are necessary for effective defence, which carries still greater risk than the legalization of anticipation.

This normative double standard is a recurring feature of normative thinking about international conflict. Defence by way of anticipation or prevention are only two examples of policies that ought to be prohibited under international law although they may be legitimate. The next section offers another example.

5 Military retaliation

Is a state ever permitted to use force in *retaliation* against an armed attack? Israeli policy may serve as an illustration. On numerous occasions in its history of conflict with Arab states and Palestinians, Israel has resorted to reprisals for guerilla operations on its territory. To take but one example, in October 1985 an Israeli air raid destroyed large parts of the headquarters of the Palestinian Liberation Organization (PLO) in Tunis. This attack was officially justified as a reaction to several terrorist assaults on Israeli citizens. Both PLO personnel and Tunisian workers and police were killed. Are actions like this justified?

One might try to make out a moral rationale by going back to John Locke's justification of harmful response to harm. It was invoked in chapter 5 as the basic premise of the right of national self-defence. Locke argues that the "safety of the innocent is to be preferred" when one person attacks another by lethal force and the latter can defend himself only by responding in kind. It seems clear that the death of the innocent person is the greater evil, which is the reason given in chapter 5 for his right to defend oneself by means of force. Not everyone, however, is content with this explanation. It may be argued that those who inflict harm on other people or set out to do so, *deserve* to suffer for their actions. Considerations of desert can be thought to underlie the idea that the worth of a person's life declines when he deliberately directs deadly force at someone else. Philip Montague (1981, p. 216) says, in particular, that it is "a matter of basic justice" that "the good and bad things that happen to people should have some reasonably direct connection with their responsible behavior". This is another way of saying that people deserve punishment that fits the wrong they have done. Montague's assumption would, if it was accepted, justify not only armed defence, but also acts of military retaliation. It implies, more generally, that the reason why people have a right of self-defence is also a reason why they may inflict harm in retaliation to aggression. If considerations of desert explain why someone weakens his claim to live by directing deadly force at another person, it follows that the use of force must always be punished. This is not to deny, of course, that harmful response to harm can have a forward-looking rationale, too. Preventing aggression may be justified in itself. But the argument above suggests that defensive measures have a more fundamental justification. At root lies the backward-looking rationale that harmful actions deserve response in kind irrespective of what instrumental purpose such response will serve.

The idea that people should be treated according to the way they behave towards others accords with the celebrated principle of respecting human autonomy. According to James Rachels (1978, p. 159), a "person who is punished for his misdeeds is *held responsible* for them in a concrete way. He is not treated as a mindless automaton, ... but as a responsible agent whose actions merit approval or resentment". However, desert is viewed by many analysts as a highly controversial basis for moral assessment. It is the subject of complex philosophical debates – much too complex to summarize here.[31] Moreover, intuitions about autonomy and responsibility in private life do not carry over directly to international relations. There is, accordingly, reason to believe that the original, forward-looking line of argument provides the most plausible rationale of the national right of self-defence.

But this need not imply that a moral permission of military retaliation cannot be grafted on to the right of self-defence. A state may resort to military retaliation for the purpose of *deterring* aggression. Retaliatory measures may, more specifically, be directed to demonstrate that external attacks will not be worth-while. In this case, punishment is not basically a question of paying harm with harm; its rationale is instrumental: to prevent future aggression. One may object, of course, that deterrence can be accomplished without actually employing means of force, by simply possessing them and making clear that they will, if necessary, be used. Sometimes, however, threats of this kind must be buttressed by force in order to be credible. According to William O'Brien, this is the case with Israel's efforts to deter terrorist activity by Palestinian groups based in neighbouring Arab countries. He says that numerous resolutions from the United Nations Security Council, which condemn Israeli actions that go beyond defence against an attack in progress, deny "the possibility of self-defence measures designed to deter future attacks which may be anticipated, based on a pattern of accumulated past attacks and good intelligence" (O'Brien 1991, p. 103).

> [C]ounterterror deterrence cannot prevent terrorist attacks in the way that nuclear and/or conventional deterrence can prevent nuclear or conventional aggression. Because of the difficulty of deterring terrorist organizations and individual terrorists from attempting terrorist operations, counterterror deterrence requires the capability and will to attack the sources of terrorism to deter its continuation. This deterrence is not based solely on the threat of unacceptable damage but the *demonstration* of unacceptable damage. (ibid.)

For Israel, O'Brien suggests, effective defence cannot be confined to fending off ongoing attacks – or, for that matter, anticipating imminent ones. The country faces an indefinite series of small-scale, isolated strikes that render normal life impossible and gradually undermine public morale. The only way of stopping them is to "attack the terrorists in the states that give them sanctuary in order to deter those states as well as the population around terrorist bases from supporting or acquiescing in terrorist operations" (ibid.).

I need not go into the empirical validity of this argument. What matters for our purpose is the possibility that a state may face the kind of threat O'Brien alludes to. The question is if it then has a moral warrant of offensive war in the form of military retaliation. It may seem so, provided retaliatory action is necessary to buttress a deterrent threat that in turn is necessary to fend off further aggression. Under such circumstances, the legitimacy of retaliation derives directly from the legitimacy of national self-defence. The assumption is that repeated attacks on national citizens can be stopped only by demonstrating national resolve and capability.

One objection immediately comes to mind. There is often no way of knowing for sure if a retaliatory attack is necessary for deterrence and defence, or if the state that makes reprisals would have been able to defend itself adequately by purely defensive means. Ample uncertainty surrounds judgments about the need to render deterrent threats credible through overt demonstrations of force. Moreover, political leaders often exaggerate the risks they face on this score. Consider, by way of example, the Athenian policy towards Mytilene in the fourth year of the Peloponnesian War, 427 BC. The city of Mytilene revolted against Athens; the Athenians crushed the revolt and "decided to put to death … the entire adult male population of Mytilene, and to make slaves of the women and children" (Thucydides 1972, bk. 3.36, p. 212). The planned punishment was cruel and indiscriminating. Many Mytilenians had not taken part in the revolt, and some who were guilty had repented. But harsh punishment was advocated on grounds of deterrence. Some Athenian leaders argued that the days of the Athenian empire would be counted if treason were treated with leniency. It "is a general rule of human nature", Cleon said, "that people despise those who treat them well and look up to those who make no concessions" (ibid., bk. 3.39, p. 215). In view of this, the Athenians were well advised to "make an example of" the Mytilenians, "plainly showing that revolt will be punished by death" (p. 217). Yet some Athenians had second thoughts. Diodotus saw a disadvantage in the indiscriminating treatment of guilty and innocent: "[W]e must not make the condition of rebels desperate by depriving them of the possibility of repentance and a chance of atoning as quickly as they can for what they did. ... [I]f Cleon's method is adopted, can you not see that every city will not only make much more careful preparations for revolt, but also hold out against siege to the very end, since to surrender early or late means just the same thing?" (p. 221)

The arguments are speculative and the disagreement hardly allows of resolution through further examination of facts. Different views of human nature support divergent estimates of the risk to Athenian security from either cruel or discriminating treatment of Mytilene. Only one thing is certain: The suggested punishment of Mytilenian citizens is in itself horrendous. It can be condoned, if at all, only if an immediate threat to Athen's survival would otherwise arise. This, however, is not the case. Cleon's view need not be deemed implausible, but the threat he conjures up is distant, and massacre is hardly its only effective remedy. His rhetoric illustrates the possibility that political leaders may magnify risks to vital interests and engage in military retaliation that has no valid rationale of deterrence.[32]

This possibility brings the vagueness argument to the fore again. Once more, we run up against Hume's qualms about the execution of laws whose proper application is surrounded by great ignorance. A war of retaliation may, under certain circumstances, be justified for defensive reasons, but a legal rule condoning this kind of war will easily lend itself to misuse. This line of argument has the same force in the present case as it had with respect to preventive war. It will be a matter of much guesswork whether or not military propensity must be demonstrated by military action in order render deterrent threats credible. Hence, a permission of retaliation easily becomes a cloak of illegitimate war. Owing to the genuine obscurity of international relations and the human propensity of self-conceit, no determinate rule of conduct will result from a permission to retaliate whenever defensive grounds of military expediency call for it.

Again, however, pragmatic considerations do not annul moral principles. A government may think that, to the best of its knowledge, national security is bound up with deterrent threats that call for military retaliation, and if so, the responsibility of trusteeship permits and obligates it to take such action. It will be justified from a moral point of view, but its legalization is too risky. This is another example of the normative double standard that came out of the discussion of defence by anticipation in section 4. Military retaliation is sometimes legitimate, but should still be pronounced illegal in order not to create a legal loophole of illegitimate retaliation.

6 Conclusion

This chapter has vindicated the legal right of national self-defence. It is a proper part of international law, but it must be defined narrowly to permit only war of pure self-defence. Wider definitions risk encouraging illegitimate uses of force. They may inspire permissive attitudes to preventive war or serve as pretexts of illegitimate retaliation. Still, the resort to force for anticipatory, preventive or retaliatory purposes may be morally permissible. The argument above grounds normative double standards that drive a wedge between moral principles and legal rules. The next chapter will do the same.

7 War of Offence: Moral Principles and Legal Rules

1 Introduction

The previous chapter asked if military attack may be undertaken for defensive purposes. I shall now consider the legitimacy and legality of war that has no defensive warrant. This is what I have in mind when I talk about war of offence. Is it ever justified?

We have registered a development towards more restrictive assumptions about *jus ad bellum*. This can be seen in both just war theory and international law. But are all kinds of offensive war really illegitimate? And should there be an absolute legal ban on the use of force for any purpose save national defence? If the first question is answered in the negative, so must the second, but not necessarily the other way round, as the previous chapter made clear. A moral permission to take up arms does not entail a legal permission to the same effect. The problem of offensive war will therefore be approached in the same way as war of defence was explored above, starting with questions of legitimacy and proceeding to legal issues. If offensive warrants of war are to be included in international law, both moral and pragmatic questions must be sorted out. First, do reasons of legitimacy call for their inclusion? Second, is their inclusion advisable when its wider implications for international relations are taken into account?

Offensive war overlaps what I have called lethal and political aggression, and it may sound strange to ask if aggression is ever legitimate. After all, the right of national defence is a correlate of the moral ban on aggression, which in turn is a corollary of the harm principle, and it seems that the existence of the right of defence rules out every permission of offensive war. Now, if it turns out that certain forms of aggression are justifiable, this may give reason to define the concept differently so that it applies only to illegitimate and illegal wars of offence. Then states will have a right of defence against all types aggression, and the question is if they also have a right to defend themselves against non-aggressive offence. Two answers are conceivable. First, conferring legitimacy on a certain kind of offensive war may mean that military defence against this kind of war is delegitimized. The reason to permit offence is at the same time a reason why defence is impermissible, and the right of defence will become a restricted right.[33] Second, a state may be permitted to attack another and the other, at the same time, permitted to defend itself by means of force. Then both parties are within their rights if they go to war – a seemingly paradoxical but by no means incomprehensible situation. People as well as states may have competitive rights which imply that one party's doing what he has a right to do creates an external impediment to the other's acting within his right (Kavka 1986, p. 300).[34]

This chapter looks at several suggestions to the effect that states are sometimes permitted to launch offensive war. These good reasons of offence will be assessed on the basis of both moral and legal considerations. Section 2 focuses on historical grievance and economic need – reasons of war that are rooted in national interests – while section 3 discusses humanitarian intervention.

2 Past injustice and present need

The most notorious example of offensive war in this century, Nazi-Germany's military invasions of other European states, is a seemingly clear case of unjustified aggression. But it was not always seen as such by everyone. Thus, the French and British policies of appeasement were partly predicated on a different conception. At the Munich Conference in September 1939, Britain and France granted Germany the right to annex the Sudetenland, and, according to one noticeable view (though not a view embraced by many Frenchmen), this right derived from the unjust treatment Germany had suffered under the Versailles Treaty that concluded World War I. Some observers saw the territorial cessions imposed on Germany in 1919 as blatant violations of legitimate claims to national self-determination. German nationals were split and made subject to alien citizenship for the purpose of placating punitive sentiments and allaying strategic concerns about European stability. In view of this, Hitler's annexation of the Sudetenland was perceived by some as a just means of liberating Czech citizens of German descent from foreign rule – less an act of aggression than an effort to rectify previous injustice.[35]

Michael Walzer (1974, pp. 88–89) calls attention to an interesting version of this argument, put forth in 1939 by a British Catholic writer, Gerald Vann. Although Vann condemns Germany's invasion of Czechoslovakia, he defends the Munich accord. While it is wrong, he says, "to commit aggression; it may be equally wrong to resist the demands that cause the aggression". The overriding concern must always be "to ensure that legitimate grievances are heard, legitimate demands satisfied" (quoted in Walzer 1974, p. 88). Germany had, in Vann's view, a just grievance and a right to forcibly assert its legitimate claims.

I shall assess neither the Versailles Treaty nor the complaints that were later raised about its infringement of German self-determination. What matters here is Vann's general view that offensive war is permissible if it is launched in response to previous violations of legitimate moral claims. The majority of lawyers, philosophers and politicians reject this view. They are at one with Justice Robert Jackson, the chief counsel for the delegation of the United States during the International Military Tribunal at Nuremberg, who stated in his opening address that "whatever grievances a nation may have, however objectionable it finds that *status quo*, aggressive warfare is an illegal means for settling those grievances or for altering those conditions" (quoted in Tucker 1960, p. 12). International law, as it stands today, echoes this position. While it condones the use of force to recover lost territory before occupation has been consolidated,[36] it sanctions practically all territorial arrangements that have proved stable for some time, even if they are the outcome of aggression and war (Cassese 1986, pp. 126–127). In this respect, the law is coarse and callous (Fleischer 1978, p. 23). It is based on rigid statutes of limitation that disregard the historical grievances of governments and people. According to the principle of prescription, territorial sovereignty always belongs to the government exercising sustained, *de facto* authority in a territory, regardless of how the territory came into its possession. An "abstract title without effective possession cannot prevail over a constant and effective manifestation of authority" (Blum 1965, p. 200).

One may ask, however, if the principle of prescription is a proper basis of international law. If people have suffered unjust treatment and ought to have their rights restored, and if force is the only effective means of restoration, is it not a legitimate resort? Does a government have to put up indefinitely with an unjust deprivation of territory because it happened to be incapable of averting it in the first place? As its citizens have been placed under foreign rule by coercive means, and the international anarchy lacks an authority to which aggrieved people can appeal for redress, are they not entitled to take the moral law into their own hands? And should not international law acknowledge their right to do so?

Before we take a closer look at this suggestion, consider another in the same vein. It has been argued, notably in Thomas Hobbes' account of poverty relief, that force may sometimes be used to acquire territory even without an intent of restoring original rights. Hobbes holds that those who "have strong bodies" ought to "maintain themselves", if necessary they should "be forced to work", and if employment cannot be had domestically, external outlets must be found.

> The multitude of poor, and yet strong people … are to be transplanted into Countries not sufficiently inhabited; where nevertheless, they are not to exterminate those they find there; but constrain them to inhabit closer together, and not range a great deal of ground, to snatch what they find; but to court each little Plot with art and labour, to give them their sustenance in due season. (Hobbes [1651] 1975, ch. 30, p. 185)

This passage does not tell whether any manner of "transplanting" poor citizens into foreign countries is permissible. Yet, the proviso about extermination indicates that harsh methods can come into question. Hobbes clearly hints at a warrant of offensive war – a principle of *jus ad bellum* that permits resort to force for the purpose of relocating people from densely to sparsely populated territories. The underlying premise is that economic subsistence matters more than territorial integrity when it comes to balancing the interests and rights of states.

Hobbes elsewhere touches on a kindred consideration that bears more directly on contemporary matters. Observing that few states are self-sufficient in material goods, he does not only mention industry and trade as remedial measures, but also – conspicuously offhand – proposes military action.

> [B]ecause there is no Territory under the Dominion of one Common-wealth, (except it be of very vast extent,) that produceth all things needfull for the maintenance, and motion of the whole Body; and few that produceth not something more than necessary; the superfluous commodities to be had within, become no more superfluous, but supply these wants at home, by importation of that which may be had abroad, either by Exchange, or by just Warre, or by Labour. (ibid., ch. 24, p. 130)

This line of argument can be made more plausible by distinguishing critical shortage of vital resources from merely inconvenient deficiency of goods which are easily available through ordinary channels of trade. One may contend that offensive war is justified if an amply equipped state refuses to let a critically deprived country procure vital goods at affordable costs. "Suppose", Jan Narveson (1980, p. 132) says, "that the rains cease to fall on country A, and that its more fortunate neighbor, B, refuses to help in various ways that it could without too great difficulty. If the starving A's now make war on the well-off B's, is this aggression?"

International law prohibits the use of force to meet economic needs, no less than it rules out forcible restoration of occupied territory. Moreover, I am not aware of any serious proposal for revising the law to legalize economic war, but when it comes to the restoration of territory, revisions have been suggested. Thus, a declaration adopted by the United Nations General Assembly in 1970, the *Principles of Friendly Relations and Cooperation among States* (resolution 2625), says that "no territorial acquisition resulting from the threat or use of force shall be recognized as legal". While this does not sanction forcible attempts to undo such acquisitions, other legal documents go further in that direction. The United Nations General Assembly Resolution 3314 says that nothing in the definition of aggression should "in any way prejudice the right of self-determination, freedom and independence ... of peoples forcibly deprived of that right ..., particularly people under colonial and racist régimes or other forms of alien domination; nor the right of these peoples to struggle to that end and to seek and receive support". Inis Claude Jr. (1980, p. 95) sees a qualification of the general ban on non-defensive military action in this passage.

> This is not an isolated bit of United Nations rhetoric, but a passage typical of a long list of resolutions ... conferring legitimacy upon wars of national liberation, wars to achieve national self-determination, wars to end racial oppression, and the like. Today, the question is not whether an act of aggression occurs, but who does it, against whom, and for what. The certified good cause converts aggression into just war.

Claude's reading of resolution 3314 is, however, idiosyncratic. There is no generally recognized development towards legal refurbishment of pre-modern doctrines of just war. But even if international law shows no sign of sanctioning "good" causes of offence, the idea of doing so hardly flies in the face of conventional morality. Elizabeth Anscombe makes the point with perfect clarity.

> [H]ow can we doubt the excellence of such a proceeding as that violent suppression of the man-stealing business which the British government took it into its head to engage in under Palmerstone? The present-day conception of "aggression", like so many other influential conceptions, is a bad one. Why *must* it be wrong to strike the first blow in a struggle? The only question is, who is in the right? (Anscombe 1971, p. 271)

It may be objected that Anscombe overlooks the distinctive nature of violence as a means of foreign policy. The resistance to distinguish between just offence and unjust aggression need not imply that all offensive wars are morally equivalent. The reason why it is wrong to strike the first blow in a struggle might rather lie in the nature of the blow itself, whose negative value always overshadows other considerations.

Recall the argument of chapter 5, which vindicated a moral right of national defence, but also revealed weighty countervailing considerations that bear on the destructiveness and indiscriminate character of every war. Doubts about the legitimacy of defensive war were raised on both consequentialist grounds pertaining to its costs in terms of death and destruction, and deontological reasons that turn on the duty not to kill innocent people. These doubts were eventually allayed, but in no confident manner. The case for a right of military defence cannot be premised on the undisputable priority of primary national interests over countervailing considerations. Moral indeterminacy and factual uncertainty often surround the choice between forcible defence and appeasement. When, however, a question of right action cannot be answered confidently, political authorities should do what is best for national citizens. This explains why they can (and should) resort to force in defence of vital national interests.

Good causes of offensive war may in principle lend themselves to the same kind of justification. War is an extraordinary evil, but if it can be let loose for defensive reasons, there may be situations in which offensive war is justified too. Endorsing defensive war is tantamount to acknowledging that the reason why someone resorts to violence makes a moral difference. There is no *inherent* evil in striking the first blow, and while the stakes involved for a nation may rarely be high enough to warrant war of offence, we have no basis for saying that they never are. Economic strangulation can, in particular, be as serious a threat to national survival as physical invasion. Whether or not the good causes discussed above are good enough to justify a state in striking the first blow depends on the circumstances. Assessments can only be had through a case by case analysis of particular conflicts.

So far, I have only discussed the legitimacy of offensive war aimed at meeting economic needs or rectifying past injustice. Next comes the question of legality. Should international law permit states to take up arms when subsistence is at stake or there is a good prospect of recovering lost territory? This question brings pragmatic concerns to the fore. What will be the effect on the quality of international relations if good causes of offence are legalized? There is a risk that the overall effect will be very adverse. A pertinent consideration on this score is the vagueness argument of chapter 4. It says that a principle that does not allow of fairly precise statement is unfit for inclusion in law if a legal rule corresponding to this principle may be used as a pretext of undesirable and illegitimate behaviour. This is clearly the case with respect to the principles underlying the good causes of offensive war discussed above. Thus, there is no way we can draw a general line between historical grievances that are weighty enough to justify a state in taking back lost territory by way of force, and grievances that do not warrant such measures. The same problem arises when it comes to economic war. David Luban (1979, pp. 176–178) suggests that "war for subsistence", in the strict sense of a "fight for life", is a legitimate war of offence, but he fears that the endorsement of this cause will serve to legitimize many others. If "we weaken the definition of unjust war to include struggles against economic collapse, the door is opened to allowing any economic war. For example, do industrialized countries have a right to go to war for OPEC oil?" (ibid.)

The problem with good causes of offensive war is, briefly put, that they spill over into bad causes. In addition to Luban's contemporary example of a war for oil, one may adduce the historical example of colonial expansion. Colonies were often portrayed as essential to the economic survival of industrialized countries around the turn of the century. Thus, the French politician Jules Ferry had an apocalyptic vision in the 1890s: "Europe's consumption is saturated: it is essential to discover new seams of consumers in other parts of the world. The alternative is to place modern society in bankruptcy and to prepare for the dawn of the 20th century in a cataclysmic social liquidation whose consequences cannot be calculated" (quoted in Fieldhouse 1976, p. 25). With hindsight, few people take this argument seriously, but it serves as a warning that conceptions of economic need vary, and the legalization of economic war opens the door to a wide variety of dubious expansionist policies.

To conclude, good causes like just grievance and economic need may provide moral rationales of war of offence. If primary national interests will otherwise be sacrificed, striking the first blow can be the right thing to do, despite the moral horror of war. But pragmatic considerations tell against revising international law to legalize any form of offensive war. A relaxation of the absolute prohibition may create pretexts of illegitimate military action. The good causes of offence do not distinguish themselves clearly from the bad ones. This argument, like the argument about anticipatory defence and retaliation in chapter 6, establishes a normative double standard. We have found another case of tension between moral considerations and pragmatic concerns which underscores that international law should not mirror morality in every respect.

3 Humanitarian intervention

We shall see one more example of the tension between morality and law in relation to yet another proposal for loosening the categorical prohibition of offensive war. According to contemporary law, all forms of *intervention* by one state in the internal affairs of another are illegal. This rule derives from the notion that each state is sovereign, which is "the basic constitutional doctrine" of international law (Brownlie 1973, p. 280). Lawyers also frequently speak of the "sovereign equality of states", by which they mean that states are on an equal footing as far as rights of domestic authority are concerned, however much they diverge in terms of size, wealth, power, prominence, and so on. Sovereignty constitutes, in effect, a defining feature of statehood. It is only natural that a system of legal norms predicated on this principle will be extremely resistant to legal provisions that may prejudice political independence.

Ian Brownlie explains that the "principal corollaries of the sovereignty and equality of states are: (1) a jurisdiction, *prima facie* exclusive, over a territory and the permanent population living there; (2) a duty of non-intervention in the area of exclusive jurisdiction of other states" (ibid.).[37] Assumptions (1) and (2) are, of course, two sides of the same coin. A right of exclusive jurisdiction entails a ban on intervention, which is to say that the right correlates with a duty of non-intervention.

I shall consider only military intervention – armed intrusion that, in James Rosenau's (1969, p. 164) oft-cited phrase, is "addressed to the authority structure of the target society – that is, to the identity of those who make the decisions that are binding for the entire society and/or to the processes through which these decisions are made". It is mostly intended to serve the interests of the intervening states, but *humanitarian* intervention differs on that score. It is a question of efforts to assist people who are being maltreated by their own government or by groups whose activities the government encourages, tolerates or at least makes no wholehearted attempt to stop. Such maltreatment has different degrees of gravity, and a distinction is often made between genocide and oppression. The former is outright slaughter of a group of people, the latter persecution, arbitrary arrest, imprisonment without fair trial, torture or starvation.

Both genocide and oppression can be opposed and stopped by other means than military interference, but it is a sad truth that diplomatic pressure, if it works at all, is a time-consuming instrument. Moreover, evacuation of victims of maltreatment is normally neither feasible nor desirable. Their government may not be willing to let them go, other countries may not be ready to receive them, and there are heavy costs to the intended beneficiaries of rescue by expatriation. Tom Farer (1973, p. 153) points to "the agony of forced separation from ancestral lands" as well as "the loss of property with the consequent trauma of a sudden, radical change in status". He concludes that "rescue, if there is to be any, will require elimination of the threat at its source. The delinquent elite must alter its policies or be removed. There must, in other words, be direct and sustained involvement in the political process of the target state". This is to say that only an assault at the center of political decision making offers immediate relief to victims of genocide and oppression.

While the principle that no sovereign state should intervene in the internal affairs of another has been a fundamental norm of international politics since World War II, some international jurists think that an exception can be made for humanitarian intervention in response to grave maltreatment of citizens by political authorities.[38] Their most important argument is that legal provisions for the protection and advancement of *human rights* qualify the strict rule of non-intervention. Such provisions figure in Article 55 of the United Nations Charter, which states that "the United Nations shall promote ... universal respect for, and observance of, human rights and fundamental freedoms for all without distinction as to race, sex, language, or religion". They have later been restated in the *Universal Declaration of Human Rights*. There is clearly a tension between these provisions and the blanket prohibition of all forms of offensive war, including intervention, that otherwise finds expression in the UN Charter. As a result, some say, the Charter "provides little guidance as to the legitimacy of 'humanitarian intervention' for the prevention of gross denial of human rights" (Moore 1974, p. xiv). It is arguable, however, that references to human rights in the UN Charter are weak (Donnelly 1984, p. 318). There is no specification of concrete steps to be taken in the face of violations, and the inference that all measures are therefore permissible would be a *non sequitur*. Moreover, the dominant opinion of governments and legal authorities echoes the strict reading of the law. It is, as Brownlie (1974, p. 219 and 218) documents, "the universal consensus of government opinion and the practice of states since 1945", so that "a jurist asserting a right of forcible humanitarian intervention has a very heavy burden of proof" (see also Brownlie 1973).

The legal prohibition notwithstanding, a good case for humanitarian intervention may be made on moral grounds: In the face of oppression or genocide that can only be stopped (within reasonable time) through foreign intervention, everyone capable of taking effective action has a duty to do so. For a simple analogue, consider the case of a person who witnesses severe maltreatment of one family member by another in the house next door. If he has reasonable prospects of bringing this to an end by entering the house, he is obligated to do so, at least as long as the costs involved fall substantially short of the costs of continued maltreatment. This follows from the weak consequentialist principle of chapter 1. Yet it does not necessarily imply that the person in question has a conclusive reasons to enter the house – that this is what he ought to do all things considered. Countervailing considerations may come into the picture here as elsewhere. The same goes for international intervention. While the weak consequentialist principle may call for military operations to protect victims of oppression or genocide, other considerations may speak against such action.

One objection derives from what we may call communitarian premises. It cautions that one cannot conclude from the nature of how a government behaves towards its citizens what attitude these citizens take towards the government. Seemingly obnoxious political arrangements may not be out of accord with popular wants and local traditions. Michael Walzer argues that foreigners have no basis for confident assessment of the "union of people and government" in a particular country.

> They don't know enough about its history, and they have no direct experience, and can form no concrete judgments, of the conflicts and harmonies, the historical choices and cultural affinities, the loyalties and resentments, that underlie it. Hence their conduct … is, or ought to be, determined … by a morally necessary presumption: that there exists a certain "fit" between the community and its government and that the state is "legitimate". (Walzer 1980, p. 212)

This view is congenial to a traditional liberal outlook on politics, with its general endorsement of tolerance and plurality and its aversion against the intrusion of fixed ideas about right and wrong on societies that differ greatly with respect to development, tradition and culture. The underlying notion is that there are many, highly divergent but equally defensible, ways of organizing social and political institutions. George Kennan (1951, p. 53) says that "[n]o people can be the judge of another's domestic institutions and requirements, and we have no need to be apologetic to anyone, unless it be ourselves, for the things we do and the arrangements we enforce within our own country". This implies, in particular, that non-democratic institutions need not be coercive and contrary to popular preferences. "Indeed, the history, culture, and religion of the community may be such that authoritarian regimes come, as it were, naturally, reflecting a widely shared world view or way of life" (Walzer 1980, pp. 224–225).

We may accept all this and still argue that humanitarian intervention is morally justified. As defined above, it is a question of military interference aimed at bringing an end to genocide or oppression, whose occurrence indicate that no "fit" exists between the community and its government. Walzer agrees, up to a point. He says that "extreme forms of oppression" overturn the presumption of communal integrity and open the door to legitimate intervention (ibid., pp. 217–218). Yet, he adds two qualifications, one intendedly and the other inadvertently. First, intervention is ruled out in the case of "ordinary" oppression, which includes everything except "massacre or enslavement". Genocide is a valid warrant of military rescue, but nothing else is. If we go by the premises of Walzer's argument, however, this distinction seems arbitrary. People who are persecuted, starved or tortured hardly stand in a communal relationship with their government – at least not one they will find worthy of preserving. While distinctions on this score can never be precise, it seems clear that Walzer's communitarian premises make room for more forms of humanitarian intervention than he endorses himself. But Walzer also, seemingly without noticing, hints at another qualification of the argument that intervention will sometimes be justified. He says that "we can always assume that murder, slavery, and mass expulsion are condemned, *at least by their victims*" (ibid., p. 218; italics added). The italicized clause alludes to the troubling fact that a genocidal or oppressive policy rarely directs itself at an entire population, but normally victimizes only a minority. In many cases, the majority of citizens are not negatively affected by the policy in question, and the union between government and citizens is intact as far as they are concerned. This partial communal integrity will be destroyed by foreign intervention. A decision must therefore be made between preserving it and intervening to rescue the minority.

Which is worst – the maltreatment of some citizens or the estrangement of others from their government? Surely, large scale massacre will have to be stopped at any expense of communal integrity, but isolated killings and sporadic occurrences of torture do not call for military intervention. The question is at what point the scales tip in favour of sacrificing an oppressed minority out of concern for a majority. All we can say is that communitarian considerations do not rule out humanitarian intervention, nor are such considerations always overridden by humanitarian concerns. Even where murder and enslavement take place, the moral costs of intervention in terms of broken communal integrity may be too high. This is disturbingly vague, but I have no confidence in more precise answers.[39]

A less compromising argument against the moral permissibility of intervention comes from John Stuart Mill. He contends that any effort to improve the political system of a state by way of external interference will be unsuccessful when it comes to installing workable, new institutions. People cannot enjoy the end-result of institutional reform without initiating and undertaking the reformation themselves. There is no short cut to political development; it must keep pace with the development of popular attitudes and understandings.

> [T]he evil is, if [people] have not sufficient love of liberty to be able to wrest it from merely domestic oppressors, the liberty which is bestowed on them by other hand than their own, will have nothing real, nothing permanent. ... When a people has had the misfortune to be ruled by a government under which the feelings and the virtues needful for maintaining freedom could not develop themselves, it is during an arduous struggle to become free by their own efforts that these feelings and virtues have the best chance of springing up. (Mill [1859] 1968, pp. 36–37)

Granted Mill's theory of political development, the case for intervention does not collapse. Humanitarian intervention is the use of force to oust tyrants, not to carry out comprehensive constitutional change. To be sure, tyrants often succumb to popular rebellion in the end, and if Mill's premises are valid, whole-scale reform is most likely to succeed if the entire reformation process is of domestic origin. But one must not overlook the costs of a long-drawn and arduous struggle for freedom. The value of self-determination notwithstanding, its optimal realization may carry an excessive price. Too many people may have to die or suffer terror and tyranny in order that virtues "needful for maintaining freedom" can arise, and genocide and severe oppression are greater evils than institutional deficiency. Thus, Mill's argument provides no conclusive case against humanitarian intervention. Like the communitarian argument, it only shows that interventionary objectives may run up against countervailing considerations and should be acted on only if the cause of intervention is so good that non-intervention would be wrong, all things considered.

If a given cause is this good, it entails a duty, not just a permission, of humanitarian intervention. This raises a new question: What if the duty to intervene runs up against the special obligation that a government has towards national citizens? What limits do national interests set to considerations of humanity? The following example shows how the two sets of concerns can collide. It relates to British policy towards Austria and Hungary on the occasion of the Hungarian nationalist revolt of 1848. This revolt, which first led to the establishment of an independent republic, was subsequently quelled by the invasion of a Russian Army, sent by Tsar Nicholas I at the request of the Austrian emperor. Liberal observers regretted Britain's passivity in this situation. They argued that the British government should have launched a counter-invasion. One proponent of this view was John Stuart Mill – a skeptic with respect to interventions that come in place of popular uprising, but an advocate of those that reinforce it.

> It might not have been right for England (even apart from the question of prudence) to have taken part with Hungary in its noble struggle against Austria ... But when, the Hungarians having shown themselves likely to prevail in this struggle, the Russian despot interposed, and joining his force to that of Austria, delivered back the Hungarians, bound hand and foot, to their exasperated oppressors, it would have been an honorable and virtuous act on the part of England to have declared that this should not be, and that if Russia gave assistance to the wrong side, England would aid the right. (Quoted in Walzer 1977, p. 93.)

What Mill calls the "question of prudence" is, I take it, the question of whether or not intervention on behalf of Hungary would accord with Britain's national interests. Mill holds that the British decision to intervene or not should be taken with due regard to these interests. Regardless of how worthy the cause of the Hungarians was, the secession of Hungary might have been a dangerous event as it would have upset the European balance of power on which British security rested. Still, Mill advocates intervention as "an honourable and virtuous act". Walzer (1977, p. 94) elaborates and comments on this view:

> [W]hether or not it actually was dangerous [to support Hungarian secession] was surely for the British to decide, and we should judge them harshly if the risks they declined to run were very slight indeed. Even if counter-intervention is "honourable and virtuous", it is not morally required, precisely because of the dangers it involves.

Walzer describes Mill's argument as directed to "the British", i.e. the people of Great Britain. In practice, however, the decision was in the hands of the British government. This implies that Mill's talk of honour and virtue, which evokes associations of discretionary duty, is out of place. The British government has no right to let its actions be guided by such considerations. Hence, Walzer directs his concern in the wrong direction. The question is not if the British people declined a slight risk, but whether or not their government would have put too much at stake by launching a counter-intervention. Given Europe's history of war and in view of the fragile balance established after 1815 amid ideological and territorial conflicts, the burden of proof is on the critics of Britain's non-intervention. But considerations of national interests do not overturn humanitarian concerns as a matter of principle. They only complicate the picture, adding another factor to be taken into account before moral decisions are made in specific situations. There remains a duty of intervening to stop genocidal or oppressive policies in the absence of overriding, countervailing considerations.

Having rebutted three prominent challenges to the moral permissibility of humanitarian intervention, we may venture to suggest that another valid warrant of offensive war has been found.[40] Let us turn, then, from questions of legitimacy to legal problems. Should international law be revised to permit humanitarian intervention? A negative answer grounded in pragmatic premises comes from Ian Brownlie. He says that humanitarian intervention raises "a moral and legislative problem of the type raised by euthanasia, itself a form of 'humanitarian intervention'. ... It is very generally assumed that legalizing euthanasia would alter the moral climate and produce harmful abuse" (Brownlie 1974, p. 223). The implication is that similar effects will ensue if humanitarian intervention is legalized. It will adversely affect the moral climate of international relations.

What specific effects does Brownlie have in mind? As far as euthanasia is concerned, he presumably envisages a weakening of the almost universal condemnation of killing in other contexts than self-defence. A permission to kill those who suffer from fatal or painful illness and desire a gentle death, may undermine respect for life in general. If euthanasia comes in a more favourable light, there is a risk that other forms of killing will do the same. The point is not, of course, that redefining euthanasia from 'prohibited' to 'permissible' logically entails a permission to kill just anyone. What Brownlie has in mind is a gradual but profound alteration of attitudes. I alluded to the underlying psychological mechanism in chapter 4. It consists in internal stress generated by legal codes whose rules are not attuned to one another. It may arise, in particular, if rules that condemn some types of premeditated murder are combined with rules that permit others. A person who is led by the law to accept the permissibility of euthanasia will become less inclined to accept a strict prohibition of killing for other purposes. Legalizing euthanasia may make it hard to understand why it is illegal and wrong to kill handicapped newborns. A reasonable analytical distinction may no doubt be drawn between the two types of killing, but it will not necessarily serve as a social barrier to illegal behaviour in the way that the categorical prohibition of killing does.

> The prohibition against killing is effective against involuntary euthanasia, but once we have accepted voluntary euthanasia, there will be no more barriers. The old, standard rule against killing is thus weakened, and the new rule which includes the exception for voluntary euthanasia will not be a defensible new barrier – or so the opponent of legalizing voluntary euthanasia might argue. (Burg 1991, p. 59)

Is this argument correct? The internal stress version of the slippery slope argument rests on empirical assumptions whose validity will be surrounded by considerable controversy in concrete cases. Thus, the hypothesis about the effect of legalizing euthanasia is speculative and debatable, but not wildly improbable. The same may be said about the hypothesis that legalizing humanitarian intervention will undermine the general prohibition of offensive war. If one type of offensive war is permitted while international law prohibits others, states *may* become reluctant to accept the remaining prohibitions, at least in full, but this is no foregone conclusion.

The chance that things go one way or the other – that internal stress arises or does not arise, triggers off or does not trigger off a change of attitude – depends on the contents of the legal rules whose combination is in question. If a legal code condones conduct that does not differ conspicuously from things the same code rules out, its permissive provisions risks detracting from the effectiveness of its restrictive ones. If, in other words, legal and illegal behaviour shade into one another, one may fear a progressive erosion of people's inhibitions towards breaking the law. It is not clear that this will be the case if international law is altered to permit humanitarian intervention, but the risk exists. Humanitarian purposes can be grouped with kindred objectives in a somewhat diffuse category of *reform intervention*. It may be asked, for example, if forcible interference to end oppression differs much from interference aimed at ending discrimination based on race, caste, religion or sex. Can the former be legalized without lowering moral inhibitions to the latter? Because the answer is uncertain, pragmatic considerations give reason to pause before the moral case for humanitarian intervention is turned into a case for weakening the legal ban on war of offence.

4 Conclusion

Initiating war is sometimes permissible from a moral point of view, but should not be permitted in international law. War of offence must, in other words, be judged by a normative double standard that allows assessments of legitimacy to diverge from assessments of legality.

Double standards always, on the face of it, represent a problem. The question is how normative evaluation should proceed if moral principles and law do not constitute coordinate premises of evaluation. If we were talking about the common problem of immoral law – legal requirements that lack moral justification and thus reflect the fallibility of legislation – the solution would be straightforward: "Legal criticisms must be taken with a grain of salt: it remains to be seen whether … the violation of law is in any respect a fault that is subject to sound criticism. That might be true in some cases, when law merits respect, but not in other cases, when law merits no respect at all" (Lyons 1984, p. 74). But this is not the way to deal with the normative double standards invoked in this chapter and the previous one. They do not reflect faulty legislation, but are knowingly adopted because we want the law to be more restrictive with respect to military action than our moral judgments are. The epilogue will look closer at this tension in normative thinking about international relations.

Epilogue Peace or Moral Order?

I have argued that international law should permit only pure self-defence because the legalization of anticipatory defence, retaliation or any type of offensive war risks undermining psychological and social barriers against an illegitimate use of force. Legitimate first strikes can be legalized only on pain of opening loopholes and creating pretexts for aggression that has no moral warrant. To avoid this, we must live with a legal code that is morally deficient in the sense that its injunctions do not mirror morality in every respect.

Assume that a state violates international law and is justified on moral grounds in doing this. It may, in particular, intervene by military force in the internal affairs of an oppressive state in order to put an end to its oppressive policies. Such intervention, like all types of intervention, is illegal, but it will be morally irreproachable if humanitarian concerns override concerns about communal integrity or other things that tend to undermine the legitimacy of intervention. Assume that this is the case – that the policy in question is illegal but legitimate. Is it, then, right or wrong – not legally or morally but *überhaupt*? What definitive assessment should we make of it?

There are three possibilities. First, we may refrain from any final assessment. The policy is illegal and legitimate, and that is that. Second, the policy may be pronounced right, all in all, because moral considerations are the ultimate court of appeal in normative matters. Third, it may be deemed wrong, all things considered, because legal rules, being justified by both moral and pragmatic considerations, reflect a more comprehensive perspective on normative questions than morality alone provides. Of these possibilities, the first is the least attractive. Only if there is no reasonable way of arriving at an overall assessment should we allow ourselves to remain of two minds. This leaves the second and the third possibility – taking either the moral or the legal point of view to be overriding. The former is the more problematic. Moral considerations figure prominently in discussion of what the law ought to be like, and it is hard to see how a normative assessment that takes only such considerations into account can overturn an assessment based on a combina-

erations into account can overturn an assessment based on a combination of moral and pragmatic concerns. It follows that an illegal but legitimate policy is, all in all, wrong.

I shall elaborate this conclusion by reference to a distinction between two functions that normative standards – legal rules as well as moral principles – can fulfill. In the first place, their invocation may be aimed at bringing about moral order – a state of affairs in which people generally behave the way they ought to do according to well-grounded moral principles. A perfect moral order is obviously beyond reach, but it makes good sense to contribute to its realization by commending or berating actions according to their rightness or wrongness. This may be called the positive function of normative argument. In the second place, normative assessment may be made with a view to discouraging only the worst forms of immorality. Its aim is not the perfection of society, but the prevention of total corruption and complete social dissolution. When this aim predominates, the *negative* aspect of normative argument is uppermost.

Both ways of arguing accord with the idea that "the general object of moral evaluation must be to contribute in some respects, by way of the actions of rational beings, to the amelioration of the human predicament – that is, of the conditions in which … rational beings, humans, actually find themselves" (Warnock 1971, p. 16). What differs is the underlying view of how serious the human predicament is and how things are liable to go wrong. Some see normative assessment and argument as a means of preserving elementary decencies in social life. Others harbour greater expectations, seeing morality and law as instruments for the creation of moral order or even vehicles of human fulfillment.

The negative aspect of morality lies, according to Stuart Hampshire (1989, p. 68), in its role in fending off the "forces of destruction". Theories that start here place the accent on "morality as prohibition and limit". The destructive forces are sinister motives and attitudes that people display in greater or lesser degree. They range from contempt and intolerance, through the urge to suppress and dominate, to sheer evil and a delight in others' suffering. The fending function of morality consists in preserving the "ordinary and elementary decencies of public life" (ibid.). The positive aspect of morality brings another interest to the fore. Under this head, morality is conceived as "aspiration and ideal" (ibid., p. 13). The object is to let loose creative forces rather than containing destructive ones. Here belong the liberal programmes of social improvement. Political institutions are measured by their contribution to the progress of civilization rather than their robustness in averting barbarism.

One may object to Hampshire's distinction that the two aspects of morality are really one, as good and evil are opposite sides of the same coin. This is, in one respect, trivially true. Moral evils are impediments to human fulfillment, and such fulfillment is possible only if destructive forces are kept at bay. But the suppression of evil is only a minimum condition of human fulfillment, and it makes a great difference to both life and moral theory how much of a challenge evil presents. If serious threats to decency and civilization are exceptional and can easily be averted, moral interest shifts to other, more lofty conditions of the good life. If, by contrast, the forces of destruction are often and strongly felt, their containment will be an overriding concern. What aspect of morality we emphasize depends, accordingly, on how we conceive different obstacles to civilization and human fulfillment. Hampshire's distinction turns on practical priorities that may compete despite the basic conceptual congruity between the two aspects.

To convey a concrete impression of the positive and the negative perspective, I shall briefly indicate how they have been put to work. The positive aspect of morality is at the center of Marxist theory. According to Jon Elster (1986), Marx's criticism of capitalism is inspired by a notion of the "best life" for human beings. He envisages a rich and variegated life that is within the reach of everyone provided social arrangements do not stifle individual development. This is the kind of argument Hampshire has in mind when he speaks of morality as aspiration and ideal. An apt contrast is Hampshire's (1978, p.11) own idea that the core of morality is a set of absolute prohibitions – "injunctions about the taking of life, about sexual relations, about the conduct of parents towards children and of children towards parents, about one's duties in times of war", and so on. Such injunctions describe "the minimum general features of a respectworthy way of life". If, say, the sanctity of life is questioned, society approximates to a "community of the subhuman" (ibid., p. 17). Moreover, the values upheld by these injunctions cannot be taken for granted. Unless confirmed by morality and law, they easily become blunted, and the result is a "callousness in policy, a dullness of sensibility," which may lead to "relapse into a state of nature" (ibid., pp. 16 and 9). Hampshire does not reject aspirations of social progress, but he fears radical decline so much that loftier considerations become practically irrelevant.

One need not go this far to understand the rationale of pronouncing anticipatory defence, retaliation and offensive war illegal and, all in all, wrong even when they are legitimate resorts to force. There exist, at present, strong moral remonstrances to the use of force save in pure self-defence. These remonstrances serve a very important negative function, contributing to preventing war – perhaps the greatest evil we know, or at least a source of the greatest evils. Sometimes, to be sure, the illegal use of force is legitimate and a necessary evil, but then, too, it must be deemed wrong if the upshot of another assessment would be to lower the normative barrier against war. Peace is more important than moral order.

Notes

1 This way of distinguishing the moral point of view leaves unclear the status of some moral-theological positions that praise and condemn actions without regard to their worldly implications, but I believe it can accommodate most secular moral thought. It also leaves open the question if it is only what we do to human beings and not, say, to animals and plants, that matters from a moral perspective. That question is irrelevant here.

2 I take a closer look at the problem of balancing moral considerations in the last section of this chapter.

3 Actually, things are a lot more complicated. In almost any non-trivial choice situation, we are more or less ignorant about the consequences of at least one alternative. Doing A_i may lead to a number of outcomes, $S_1, S_2, \ldots, S_n$, and we do not know which. It may result in both desirable and detestable states of affairs. If so, some would say, the rational thing to do – and, hence, the right way to discharge a consequentialist duty – is to opt for the alternative which promises to produce the highest expected value. Let $U(S_j)$ denote the value or *utility* of S_j, as judged by the pertinent value criterion, and $P(S_j/A_i)$ be the probability of S_j given A_i. A consequentialist might say that one ought to act so as to maximize $\sum U(S_j) \cdot P(S_j/A_i)$, for all *i* and *j*. There is, however, doubt about maximization of expected value as a standard of rational action under ignorance. Knowledge about probabilities may be too unreliable to sustain the requisite calculations, and perhaps some outcomes are so dreadful that one should shun any action that risks producing them, however high its expected value.

4 It should be mentioned that Scanlon (1982, pp. 110ff) eventually rejects philosophical utilitarianism in favour of another basis of moral thinking. He takes the core of morality to be a requirement that we act towards other people in conformity with rules which they could not reasonably reject as part of an unforced and informed agreement on how social behaviour is to be regulated. The point is that no one should suffer treatment that they would not freely and rationally consent to undergo.

5 A moral outlook that takes only negative duties into account has an air of arbitrariness to it. How can we acknowledge a duty to forbear harmful conduct and at the same time not feel bound to help victims of harmful conduct? Reasons of coherence might suggest that the harm principle be supplemented by positive requirements that shift the focus from duties of restraint to duties of benevolence. This is not, however, an issue in this book.

6 A stark statement of impersonal and impartial morality is William Godwin's conception of justice as "no respecter of persons". We are, he says, "not connected with one or two percipient beings, but with a society, a nation, and in some sense with the whole family of mankind" (Godwin [1798] 1976, bk. II, p. 169).

7 I have adopted this terminology from Shelly Kagan (1989, p. 17), who writes: "The term 'pro tanto' may be somewhat unfamiliar (partially, perhaps, because my use of it is also slightly ungrammatical), so a word of explanation may be in order. A *pro tanto* reason has genuine weight, but nonetheless may be outweighed by other considerations. Thus, calling a reason a pro tanto reason is to be distinguished from calling it a *prima facie* reason, which I take to involve an epistemological qualification: a prima facie reason *appears* to be a reason, but may actually not be a reason at all, or may not have weight in all cases it appears to. In contrast, a pro tanto reason is a genuine reason – with actual weight – but it may not be a *decisive* one in various cases."

8 It is an open question, however, whether Sidgwick (op. cit., p. 77) is right that the best way to "free from error the apparent cognition that most men have of the rightness or reasonableness of conduct", is to go to such lengths as he did himself in importing "method" and "rational procedure" into ethical thinking. To reflect on moral problems at a distance and with a calm mind, is not obviously the proper way of dealing with them. It may be, by contrast, that "[t]o think seriously of moral matters is not so much to ... fix our common intuitions and principles, as to force ourselves to reflect on these [matters] out of a living sense of the pathos, the violence, the intensity, the conviction, the contingency, the risk and contest of morally opposed forces" (Margolis 1979, p. 744).

9 This assertion was made more than three decades after Kennan left the foreign service, but it reiterates and elaborates opinions he had arrived at in the early 1950s: "When the individual's behavior passes through the machinery of political organization ... to find its expression in the actions of a government, then it undergoes a general transmutation, and the same moral concepts are no longer relevant to it. A government is an agent, not a principal; and no more than any other agent may it attempt to be the conscience of its principal" (Kennan 1954, p. 48).

10 G.W.F. Hegel is said to have held a somewhat different version of the view that moral considerations are irrelevant to normative assessments of foreign policy. "For Hegel," E.H. Carr ([1946] 1958, p. 153) writes, "states are complete and morally self-sufficient entities; and relations between them express only the concordance or conflict of independent wills not united by any mutual obligation." This interpretation is echoed by F.H. Hinsley (1986, p. 208), who speaks of Hegel's "conception of the state as the realization of the moral idea and as an absolute end; of his insistence that, since there is no other law for the state but the purpose of its own self, the relation between states must be a relation of 'independencies' which may stipulate among themselves but which remain above all stipulations".

11 The second argument is elaborated by Haskel Fain (1972, p. 25) with particular reference to military obligations: "I do not believe one can be morally indifferent to *any* of one's actual obligations – if one has a *military* obligation, for example, to obey one's superior officer, and soldiers do, then that obligation has *some* relative moral weight, however minuscule, in determining whether, say, a soldier should obey an order to shoot unarmed civilians. If you don't fancy that kind of moral equation, then abolish the institution that can give even the commands of near-morons moral weight in matters of life and death."

12 The two meanings of 'interest' correspond closely to the two notions of 'well-being' that were defined in chapter 1. I then argued that we may determine how well a person fares either by registering his subjective appreciation of his situation, or by ascertaining how highly he scores on some fixed scale of well-being, say, life-expectancy or state of health. Still, fulfilling personal interests is not equivalent to being well. Interests relate to everything a person cares about or is affected by, while well-being depends only on things that make him better or worse off. Thus, "[a]n agent may take an interest in the welfare of another person ... even though he does not expect that person's well-being to lead to a more immediately personal benefit for the agent himself" (Kagan 1989, p. 234). Sometimes, moreover, a person takes an interest in doing things that adversely affect his well-being, both subjectively and objectively defined. He may, e.g., work so hard to fulfill academic ambitions that he is always exhausted and ruins his health.

13 A notable exception is President Charles de Gaulle, who said: "I am not concerned with the happiness of the French. One dies for France. That proves that there is something different from and bigger than the French." William Pfaff, from whom I quote this remark (*International Herald Tribune*, June 16–17, 1990), comments: "[De Gaulle] was indifferent to democratic opinion; his obligation was to a nation. The people's representatives had put Marshal Pétain in power, and the French people in 1940 almost certainly would have voted for the marshal and for collaboration with the German occupation, or at least for peaceful acceptance of it. They certainly would not have voted for de Gaulle."

14 One may also, of course, ask if there are good reasons to think well of democracy in the first place, but I shall assume that there are and dodge this question. In any case, democratic principles are closely linked to the idea that a government is the trustee of national citizens.

15 In Malnes (1988), I discuss the moral and political problems involved in overruling someone's opinion on the grounds that he is not in his right mind.

16 Kennan recently affirmed this view with reference to the "general acceptance by Congress and the public" of the United States' military intervention in Somalia in December 1992. He sees it as "an emotional reaction, not a thoughtful or deliberate one", andcontinues: "if American policy from here on out ... is to be controlled by popular emotional impulses ... then there is no place - not only for myself, but for what have traditionally been regarded as the responsible deliberative organs of our government, in both executive and legislative branches" (*International Herald Tribune*, 1 October 1993).

17 This depiction of the situation presupposes that interests can be ranked on a fixed scale of importance, which is not a very bold assumption. "The loss of a leg," Adam Smith ([1759] 1976, p. 29) says, "may generally be regarded as a more real calamity than the loss of a mistress", and the loss of life is worse than economic hardships. As we move further down the scale of seriousness, such comparisons will become more debatable, but the notion that a scale exists is beyond controversy. Not only individual interests but even national interests can be compared with respect to urgency. This point is related to what I said in chapter 2 about the special status of security, integrity and prosperity among national interests. Moreover, it brings back a problem that arose in that connection. It may appear that the idea of comparing interests in terms of urgency is at odds with liberal and democratic respect for subjective preferences. Can we say, *a priori*, that some interests are more important than others without denying, or at least diluting, this kind of respect? Not necessarily. On the one hand, the fact that life is in itself more important than, say, honour, does not debar a person from staking health in the pursuit of fame. He may, f.ex., choose to become a martyr rather than protecting himself from a would–be murderer. On the other hand, a person cannot use just any scale for *interpersonal* comparison of interests. Regardless of how he ranks his own life and honour in terms of relative importance, his honour does not count for more than another person's life. On the latter score, what counts is the objective ranking of different interests, not their subjective ranking by particular people.

18 Some might object that a duty exists under special circumstances – if, say, the two persons are a father and his child – but I shall disregard such complications here. We may think of the two shipwrecked persons as complete strangers.

19 Michael Howard defines force as "violence [used] with great deliberation" (1979, p. 3; italics deleted). War, he says, "consists of ... deliberate, controlled, and purposeful acts of force combined and harmonized to attain what are ultimately political objectives" (ibid.).

20 Broad generalizations like this are, of course, not the whole story. J.T. Johnson (1975) points to some notable anomalies. On the one hand, the Catholic church of the Middle Ages did not rest its official case for crusades against the infidels exclusively, or even primarily, on the offensive warrant of holy war. In contrast, "the papally accepted apologetic for the crusades always strongly emphasized the temporal injustices perpetrated by the infidels upon nations and pilgrims who just happened to be Christian" (ibid., p. 51). On the other hand, a philosopher commonly noted for his modernity, Francis Bacon, gives pride of place to holy war in his theory of *justum bellum* (*ibid.*, pp. 93–94).

21 The following account draws on Malnes (1992a, pp. 295–297).

22 Good accounts of the general form of the argument are found in Glover (1977, pp. 165 – 167), Govier (1982) and Williams (1985 a).

23 The example is inspired by Govier (1982, pp. 310–311).

24 It may be argued that the relevant choice is not between military defence and appease ment, but between military defence, non-violent defence and appeasement. There are, in other words, ways of defending national sovereignty that do not involve means of

force. The population may, for example, resort to large-scale civilian disobedience in order to frustrate the objectives of an invader. Still, with strategies of non-violence still in an undeveloped and largely untried state, the crucial choice when it comes to putting up serious resistance is whether or not to take up arms.

25 The principle of moderation is sometimes expressed as a rule of proportionality. It says that a military campaign should not take place if the foreseeable costs, measured primarily by deaths and destruction, are out of proportion to the objective of the campaign. This rule is reminiscent of the disproportionality argument that was discussed in section 4. The difference is that that argument has to do with the overall consequences of war while we are now talking about costs pertaining to concrete military campaigns. The rule of proportionality says that no military action should be undertaken if its expected value does not surpass its costs in terms of suffering and devastation.

26 The Gulf War of 1992, which liberated Kuwait from Iraqi occupation, has been mentioned as an exception to the rule. Bernard E. Trainor approvingly contrasts the conduct of allied forces under American command to American operations in Vietnam (*International Herald Tribune*, 23 January, 1992). He argues that the Gulf War marked the point where technology "catch[ed] up with the doctrine of precision bombing. ... [P]recision-guided weapons eradicated targets in central Baghdad while leaving surrounding structures intact. ... Iraq's ability to wage war was crippled without accompanying civilian slaughter". The last characterization seems apt, but there are strong indications that the former may be wrong. The destruction of social infrastructure in Baghdad and elsewhere was serious and appears to have disrupted water systems and other important civilian services, like health care, resulting in a serious health crisis.

27 Roger Ruston (1984, p. 55) offers an argument for deflating patriotist sentiments as grounds of guilt. He says that patriotism "is, after all, something which the individual member of a modern nation-state can hardly avoid". This argument tends, however, to prove too much if we are to preserve the distinction between combatants and non-combatants. Many nationalist attitudes that dispose people to active military service also seem unavoidable in a modern nation-state, which is to say that even soldiers can qualify as innocents on Ruston's premises.

28 Vattel quotes his philosophical mentor, Christian Wolff, who held that "[n]ations can only be considered as so many individual persons living together in a state of nature, and therefore all the duties and the rights which nature prescribes and imposes upon all men, ... should be applied to States as well" (Vattel [1758] 1970, vol. III, p. 94). Vattel believes, moreover, that they normally are so applied, as public policy displays "calmness and deliberation" and is not "determined by the blind rashness or the whim of an individual" (p. 98).

29 This is not to say that pragmatism à la Vattel was the major reason why international lawyers abandoned principles of *jus ad bellum*. There was also talk about a *compétence de guerre* that many believed to inhere in national sovereignty much as rights of domestic legislation do (Hinsley, 1986, p. 209). This notion went further than Vattel's tactical concession to the political necessity of legalizing war with a view to restraining it. It implied that each government is morally free to take up arms whenever national interests require. The idea of *compétence de guerre* amounts, in other words, to a principled rejection of moral distinctions between just and unjust objectives of war.

30 The slippery slope may have another dimension as well. The relaxation of legal provisions on self-defence may not only provide a disguise of preventive measures against remote threats of aggression, but also of military action beyond national territory. Certain states have, indeed, claimed this kind of geographically extended right of self-defence. Great Britain invoked the following reservation to the Kellogg–Briand Pact of 1928: "There are certain regions of the world the welfare of which constitutes a special and vital interest for our peace and safety. ... Their protection against attack is to the British Empire a measure of self-defence" (quoted in Fawcett 1982, p. 27). It seems clear, however, that a permission of anticipatory attack does not lend itself to camouflaging action beyond national territory with the same ease that it can serve to disguise preventive war.

31 George Sher (1987) undertakes a detailed, if inconclusive, discussion of desert as a basis for determining what treatment people are entitled to in various contexts. Recent debate on this issue is largely spurred by John Rawls (1971), who holds that considerations of desert cannot serve as an ultimate premise for moral assessment.

32 In this case, excesses were avoided. Diodotus' appeal for leniency was eventually heeded, although the margins were narrow. To the very last, the Athenians "held conflicting opinions, and at the show of hands the votes were nearly equal. However, the motion of Diodotus was passed" (Thucydides 1972, bk. 3.49, p. 222).

33 Jeremy Waldron (1981, p. 31) points out that the statement that an agent "has a moral right to perform a particular action A never stands on its own"; it presupposes that A "is a member of a certain set of actions any of which P has the right to perform in the circumstances". It would be misleading to speak of a right if it did not have this property of generality – if, that is, A was the only option permitted and protected by the right. Generality is, however, a matter of degree. Most rights protect some, but not all, options within the boundaries of permissible action that they establish. The right of political association is an example. On the conventional view, it entitles people to join political parties of various ideological bents, or no party at all, but it does not license membership in racist or terrorist organizations. It is a general but restricted right, and so may the right of national defence be.

34 This, according to H.L.A. Hart (1967, p. 57), may be the situation in "those areas of social life where competition is at least morally unobjectionable. Two people walking along both see a ten-dollar bill in the road twenty yards away, and there is no clue as to the owner. Neither of the two are under a 'duty' to allow the other to pick it up; each has in this sense a right to pick it up".

35 This is not to say that such considerations provided the major motive behind British and French appeasement, and there were, William Keylor (1984, pp. 174–175) argues, "those in England and France who were willing to tolerate and even to encourage the diversion of Germany's expansionist energies eastward at the expense of states for which they had little concern".

36 This qualification provides a plausible, if not undisputed, legal justification of Britain's military action to take back the Falklands Islands from Argentina in 1982. James Turner Johnson (1986, p. 34) adduces the Falklands conflict as "an instructive contemporary example" of the "allowance of after-the-fact use of force to regain something wrongly taken". But some analysts, like Christoph Bluth (1987, pp. 9–12), reject the legality of the British counter-invasion of the islands.

37 Brownlie also mentions a third corollary, which is that states incur legal obligations only if they consent to legal rules, but that need not concern us here.

38 See, for example, the conference-proceedings recorded in Lillich (1973, pp. 3–138).

39 Charles Krauthammer writes (*International Herald Tribune*, 12–13 December 1992): "One murder is a crime. A million murders is a crime against humanity. Genocide is the end not just of life, but of history, memory, posterity." This is to suggest that the crucial issue is not the amount of suffering an oppressive policy brings about, but its implications for the continued existence of culturally defined groups. Krauthammer's distinction lowers the risk of excessive interventionism, but only at the cost of tolerating many personal tragedies.

40 There are, of course, other objections to humanitarian intervention. It has been pointed out, for example, that states never intervene for unselfish purposes. Some events come to mind, like the French intervention in Syria in 1860 to "save the Christian Maronite tribes of the Lebanon from the ravages of the Moslem Druses" (Vincent 1974, p. 11), but acts of "pure humanity" are extremely rare, and ulterior considerations are normally the real motives of military intervention. This suggests that its victims will almost invariably be weak states, which introduces an element of "systematic discrimination" in the picture (Donnelly 1984, p. 321). Such discrimination is regrettable, but hardly a reason to say that humanitarian intervention is always impermissible. The fact that all victims of genocidal and oppressive policies cannot be saved does not diminish the importance of saving those who can.

References

Acheson, Dean. 1967. Ethics in international relations today. In M.G. Raskin and B.B. Fall (eds.): *The Viet-Nam Reader*. New York: Vintage Books.

Anscombe, G.E.M. 1971. War and murder. In James Rachels (ed.): *Moral Problems*. New York: Harper.

(Aquinas, Thomas.) 1967. *Thomas Aquinas*. (Excerpts edited by Knut Erik Tranøy.) Oslo: Pax.

(Aquinas, Thomas.) 1988. *St. Thomas Aquinas on Politics and Ethics*. New York: W.W. Norton.

Aristotle. 1986. *The Politics*. Harmondsworth: Penguin.

Augustine. 1962. Reply to Faustus. Excerpts in *The Political Writings*. Chicago: Gateway.

Augustine. 1962a. Letters. Excerpts in *The Political Writings*. Chicago: Gateway.

Austin, John. [1832] 1954. *The Province of Jurisprudence Determined*. London: Weidenfeld and Nicholson.

Barry, Brian. 1965. *Political Argument*. London: Routledge and Kegan Paul.

Barry, Brian. 1967. The public interest. In Anthony Quinton (ed.): *Political Philosophy*. Oxford: Oxford University Press.

Beitz, Charles R. 1979. *Political Theory and International Relations*. Princeton, NJ: Princeton University Press.

Blum, Yehuda Z. 1965. *Historic Titles in International Law*. The Hague: Nijhoff.

Bluth, Christopher. 1987. The British resort to force in the Falkland/Malvinas conflict 1982. *Journal of Peace Research*, 24, 1, 5–20.

Brodie, Bernard. 1959. *Strategy in the Missile Age*. Princeton, NJ: Princeton University Press.

Brodie, Bernard. 1973. *War and Politics*. London: Casell.

Brownlie, Ian. 1968. *International Law and the Use of Force by States*. Oxford: Clarendon Press.

Brownlie, Ian. 1973. *Principles of Public International Law*. Oxford: Clarendon Press.

Brownlie, Ian. 1974. Humanitarian intervention. In John Norton Moore (ed.): *Law and Civil War in the Modern World*. Baltimore: Johns Hopkins University Press.

Buhite, Russel D. and Hamel, W.M. Christopher. 1990. War for peace: The question of an American preventive war against the Soviet Union, 1945–1955. *Diplomatic History*, 14, 3, 367–384.

Bull, Hedley. 1966. The Grotian conception of international society. In H. Butterfield and M. Wight (eds.): *Diplomatic Investigations*. London: Allen and Unwin.

Burg, Wibren van der. 1991. The slippery slope argument. *Ethics*, 102, 1, 42–65.

Carr, E.H. [1946] 1958. *The Twenty Years' Crisis 1919–1939*. London: Macmillan.

Cassese, Antonio. 1986. *International Law in a Divided World*. Oxford: Clarendon Press.

Claude, Inis., L, Jr. 1980. Just wars: Doctrines and institutions. *Political Science Quarterly*, 95, 1, 83–96.

Cohen, Marshall. 1984. Moral skepticism and international relations. *Philosophy and Public Affairs*, 13, 4, 299–346.

D'Amato, Anthony A. 1971. *The Concept of Custom in International Law*. Ithaca, NY: Cornell University Press.

Dancy, Jonathan. 1993. *Moral Reasons*. Oxford: Basil Blackwell.

Donnelly, Jack. 1984. Human rights, humanitarian intervention and American foreign policy: Law, morality and politics. *Journal of International Affairs*, 37, 2, 311–328.

Downie, R.S. 1964. *Government Action and Morality*. London: Macmillan.

Dummett, Michael. 1984. Nuclear warfare. In Nigel Blake and Kay Poole (eds.): *Objections to Nuclear Deterrence*. London: Routledge and Kegan Paul.

Eden, Anthony. 1960. *Full Circle*. London: Cassell.

Elbe, Joachim von. 1939. The evolution of the concept of the just war in international law. *The American Journal of International Law*, 33, 665–688.

Elster, Jon. 1986. Self-realization in work and politics: The Marxist conception of the good life. *Social Philosophy and Policy*, 3, 2, 97–126.

(Erasmus of Rotterdam.) [1517] 1964. The Complaint of Peace. In *The Essential Erasmus*. New York: Meridian.

Evera, Stephen Van. 1986. Why cooperation failed in 1914. In Kenneth A. Oye (ed.): *Cooperation under Anarchy*. Princeton, NJ: Princeton University Press.

Fain, Haskell. 1972. The idea of the state. *Nous*, 6, 1, 15–26.

Farer, Tom J. 1973. Humanitarian intervention: The view from Charlottesville. In Richard B. Lillich (ed.): *Humanitarian Intervention and the United Nations*. Charlottesville, Va.: University Press of Virginia.

Fawcett, James. 1982. *Law and Power in International Relations*. London: Faber and Faber.

Fieldhouse, D.K. 1976. *Economics and Empire 1830–1914*. London: Weidenfeld & Nicolson.

Fishkin, James S. 1982. *The Limits of Obligation*. New Haven, Conn.: Yale University Press.

Fleischer, Carl August. 1978. *Hovedpunkter i folkeretten* (Main Elements of International Law). Oslo: Universitetsforlaget.

Ford, John C. [1944] 1970. The morality of obliteration bombing. In Richard A. Wasserstrom (ed.): *War and morality*. Belmont, Calif.: Wadsworth.

Franck, Thomas M. 1970. Who killed Article 2(4)? Changing norms governing the use of force by states. *American Journal of International Law*, 64, 2, 809–837.

Frankel, Joseph. 1970. *National Interest*. London: Macmillan.

Glover, Jonathan. 1977. *Causing Death and Saving Life*. Harmondsworth: Penguin.

Godwin, William. [1798] 1976. *Enquiry Concerning Political Justice*. Harmondsworth: Penguin.

Good, Robert C. 1965. National interest and moral theory: The "debate" among contemporary political realists. In R. Hilsman and R.C. Good (eds.): *Foreign Policy in the Sixties: The Issues and Instruments*. Baltimore: Johns Hopkins University Press.

Govier, Trudy. 1982. What's wrong with slippery slope arguments? *Canadian Journal of Philosophy*, 12, 2, 303–316.

Grotius, Hugo. [1625] 1970. *De jure belli ac pacis*. Excerpts in M.G. Forsyth, H.M.A. Keens-Soper and P. Savigaar (eds.): *The Theory of International Relations. Selected Texts*. London: Allen and Unwin.

Hampshire, Stuart. 1978. Morality and pessimism. In Stuart Hampshire (ed.): *Public and Private Morality*. Cambridge: Cambridge University Press.

Hampshire, Stuart. 1989. *Innocence and Experience*. London: Allen Lane.

Hare, J.E. and Joynt, Carey B. 1982. *Ethics and International Affairs*. London: Macmillan.

Hare, R.M. 1979. *Moral Thinking. Its Levels, Method and Point*. Oxford: Clarendon Press.

Hart, H.L.A. 1967. Are there any natural rights? In Anthony Quinton (ed.): *Political Philosophy*. Oxford: Oxford University Press.

Hart, H.L.A. 1986. *Law, Liberty and Morality*. Oxford: Oxford University Press.

Heyd, David. 1982. *Supererogation. Its Status in Ethical Theory*. Cambridge: Cambridge University Press.

Hinsley, F.H. 1986. *Sovereignty*. Cambridge: Cambridge University Press.

Hirschman, Albert O. 1977. *The Passions and the Interests. Political Arguments for Capitalism before its Triumph*. Princeton, NJ: Princeton University Press.

Hobbes, Thomas. [1651] 1975. *Leviathan*. London: Dent.

Hoffmann, Stanley. 1981. *Duties Beyond Borders. On the Limits and Possibilities of Ethical International Politics*. Syracuse, NY: Syracuse University Press.

Howard, Michael. 1979. Temperamenta Belli: Can war be controlled? In Michael Howard (ed.): *Restraints on War*. Oxford: Oxford University Press.

Hume, David. [1777] 1975. *Enquiries Concerning Human Understanding and Concerning the Principles of Morals*. Oxford: Clarendon Press.

Johnson, James Turner. 1973. Toward reconstructing the jus ad bellum. *The Monist*, 57, 4, 461–488.

Johnson, James Turner. 1975. *Ideology, Reason, and the Limitation of War. Religious and Secular Concepts 1200–1740*. Princeton, NJ: Princeton University Press.

Johnson, James Turner. 1981. *The Just War Tradition and the Restraint of War. A Moral and Historical Inquiry*. Princeton, NJ: Princeton University Press.

Johnson, James Turner. 1986. Threats, values, and defense: Does the defense of values by force remain a moral possibility? In William V. O'Brien and John P. Langan (eds.): *The Nuclear Dilemma and the Just War Tradition*. Lexington: Lexington Books.

Kagan, Shelly. 1989. *The Limits of Morality*. Oxford: Clarendon Press.

Kavka, Gregory S. 1984. Nuclear deterrence: Some moral perplexities. In Douglas MacLean (ed.): *The Security Gamble*. Totowa, NJ: Rowman and Allanheld.

Kavka, Gregory S. 1986. *Hobbesian Moral and Political Theory*. Princeton, NJ: Princeton University Press.

Kennan, George F. 1951. *American Diplomacy 1900–1950*. Chicago: University of Chicago Press.

Kennan, George F. 1954. *Realities of American Foreign Policy*. Princeton, NJ: Princeton University Press.

Kennan, George F. 1985/86. Morality and foreign policy. *Foreign Affairs*, 64, 2, 205–218.

Keylor, William R. 1984. *The Twentieth-Century World. An International History*. New York: Oxford University Press.

Krasner, Stephen D. 1978. *Defending the National Interest*. Princeton, NJ: Princeton University Press.

Lackey, Douglas. 1984. *Moral Principles and Nuclear Weapons*. Totowa, NJ: Rowman and Allanheld.

Lauterpacht, Hersch 1946. The Grotian tradition in international law. In *British Yearbook of International Law*, 1–54.

Lichtenberg, Judith 1981. National boundaries and moral boundaries: A cosmopolitan view. In Peter G. Brown (ed.): *Boundaries. National Autonomy and Its Limits*.Totowa, NJ: Rowman and Littlefield.

Lillich, Richard B. (ed.). 1973: *Humanitarian Intervention and the United Nations*. Charlottesville, Va.: University Press of Virginia.

Lipson, Leon. 1975. International law. In Fred I. Greenstein and Nelson W. Polsby (eds.): *Handbook of Political Science*. Vol. 8. *International Politics*. Reading, Mass.: Addison-Wesley.

Locke, John. [1690] 1984. *Two Treatises of Government*. London: Dent.

Luban, David. 1979. Just war and human rights. *Philosophy and Public Affairs*, 9, 2, 160–181.

Lyons, David. 1984. *Ethics and the Rule of Law*. Cambridge: Cambridge University Press.

McCoubrey, Hilaire and White, Nigel D. 1992. *International Law and Armed Conflict*. Aldershot: Dartmouth.

Machiavelli, Niccolò. [1531] 1975. *The Prince*. Glasgow: Fontana Books.

Mackie, J.L. 1975. Causes and conditions. In E. Sosa (ed.): *Causation and Conditions*. London: Oxford University Press.

Malnes, Raino. 1988. Popular sovereignty and good government: A tension in contract theory and a liberal dilemma. In Dag Anckar, Hanni Nurmi and Matti Wiberg (eds.): *Rationality and Legitimacy*. Helsinki: The Finnish Political Science Association.

Malnes, Raino. 1992. Philsophical argument and political practice: On the methodology of normative theory. *Scandinavian Political Studies,* 15, 2, 117–134.

Malnes, Raino. 1992a. Norms under anarchy: The case of international law. In Raino Malnes and Arild Underdal (eds.): *Rationality and Institutions.* Oslo: Scandinavian University Press.

Malnes, Raino. 1993. *The Hobbesian Theory of International Conflict.* Oslo: Scandinavian University Press.

Margolis, Joseph. 1979. The prospects of an objective morality. *Social Research,* 46, 4, 744–765.

Mavrodes, George I. 1975. Conventions and the morality of war. *Philosophy and Public Affairs,* 4, 2, 117–131.

Meinecke, Friedrich. [1924] 1962. *Machiavellism.* London: Routledge and Kegan Paul.

Mill, John Stuart. [1859] 1968. A few words on non-intervention. In Richard A. Falk (ed.): *The Vietnam War and International Law,* Vol. 1. Princeton, NJ: Princeton University Press.

Montague, Philip. 1981. Self-defense and choosing between lives. *Philosophical Studies,* 40, 4, 207–219.

Moore, John Norton. 1974. Toward an applied theory for the regulation of intervention. In John Norton Moore (ed.): *Law and Civil War in the Modern World.* Baltimore: Johns Hopkins University Press.

Morgenthau, Hans J. 1951. *In Defense of the National Interest.* New York: Alfred Knopf.

Morgenthau, Hans J. 1968. *Politics among Nations.* New York: Alfred Knopf.

Murphy, Jeffrie G. 1973. The killing of the innocent. *The Monist,* 57, 4, 527–550.

Nagel, Thomas. 1978. Ruthlessness in public life. In Stuart Hampshire (ed.): *Public and Private Morality.* Cambridge: Cambridge University Press.

Nardin, Terry. 1983. *Law, Morality, and the Relations of States.* Princeton, NJ: Princeton University Press.

Narveson, Jan. 1980. Violence and war. In Tom Regan (ed.): *Matters of Life and Death.* Philadelphia: Temple University Press.

Niemeyer, Gerhart. 1941. *Law Without Force. The Function of Politics in International Law.* Princeton, NJ: Princeton University Press.

O'Brien, William V. 1991. *Law and Morality in Israel's War with the PLO.* London: Routledge.

Quester, George H. 1977. *Offense and Defense in the International System.* New York: John Wiley.

Rachels, James. 1978. What people deserve. In John Arthur and William Shaw (eds.): *Justice and Economic Distribution.* Englewood Cliffs, NJ: Prentice Hall.

Ramsey, Paul. 1961. *War and the Christian Conscience.* Durham, NC: Duke University Press.

Ramsey, Paul. 1968. *The Just War: Force and Political Responsibility.* New York: Charles Scribner's Sons.

Rawls, John. 1971. *A Theory of Justice.* London: Oxford University Press.

Roose, Frank De. 1990. Self-defence and national defence. *Journal of Applied Philosophy,* 7, 2, 159–169.

Rosenau, James N. 1969. Intervention as a scientific concept. *Journal of Conflict Resolution*, 13, 1, 149–171.

Ruston, Roger. 1984. Nuclear deterrence and the use of the just war doctrine. In Nigel Blake and Kay Poole (eds.): *Objections to Nuclear Deterrence*. London: Routledge and Kegan Paul.

Scanlon, Thomas M. 1975. Preference and urgency. *Journal of Philosophy*, 72, 655–670.

Scanlon, Thomas M. 1982. Contractualism and utilitarianism. In Amartya Sen and Bernard Williams (eds.): *Utilitarianism and Beyond*. Cambridge: Cambridge University Press.

Schlesinger, Arthur, Jr. 1972. National interests and moral absolutes. In W.W. Lefever (ed.): *Ethics and World Politics*. Baltimore: Johns Hopkins University Press.

Schweller, Randall L. 1992. Domestic structure and preventive war. Are democracies more pacific? *World Politics*, 44, 1, 235–269.

Sen, Amartya K. 1979. Utilitarianism and welfarism. *Journal of Philosophy*, 76, 9, 463–489.

Sher, George. 1987. *Desert*. Princeton, NJ: Princeton University Press.

Sidgwick, Henry. [1907] 1981. *The Methods of Ethics*. Indianapolis: Hackett Publishing Company.

Simmons, A. John. 1979. *Moral Principles and Political Obligations*. Princeton, NJ: Princeton University Press.

Singer, Peter. 1979. *Practical Ethics*. Cambridge: Cambridge University Press.

Smart, J.J.C. 1973. An outline of a system of utilitarian ethics. In J.J.C. Smart and Bernard Williams (eds.): *Utilitarianism – For and Against*. London: Cambridge University Press.

Smith, Adam. [1759] 1976. *The Theory of Moral Sentiments*. Oxford: Clarendon Press.

Sterling, Richard W. 1965. Political necessity and moral principle in the thought of Friedrich Meinecke. In R. Hilsman and R.C. Good (eds.): *Foreign Policy in the Sixties: The Issues and Instruments*. Baltimore: Johns Hopkins University Press.

Stocker, Michael. 1970. Moral duties, institutions, and natural facts. *The Monist*, 54, 4, 602–624.

Stone, Julius. 1958. *Aggression and World Order. A Critique of United Nations Theories of Aggression*. London: Stevens.

Swanton, Christine. 1980. The concept of interests. *Political Theory*, 8, 1, 83–101.

Teichman, Jenny. 1986. *Pacifism and the Just War*. Oxford: Basil Blackwell.

Thomson, Judith Jarvis. 1991. Self-defence. *Philosophy and Public Affairs*, 20, 4, 283–310.

Thucydides. 1972. *The Peloponnesian War*. Harmondsworth: Penguin.

Tractenberg, Marc. 1988/89. A "wasting asset". American strategy and the shifting nuclear balance, 1949–1954. *International Security*, 13, 3, 5–49.

Trianosky, Gregory W. 1978. Rule-utilitarianism and the slippery slope. *Journal of Philosophy*, 125, 8, 414–424.

Tucker, Robert W. 1960. *The Just War*. Baltimore: Johns Hopkins University Press.

Vattel, Emmerich de. [1758] 1970. The law of nations. Excerpts in M.G. Forsyth, H.M.A. Keens-Soper and P. Savigaar (eds.): *The Theory of International Relations. Selected Texts*. London: Allen and Unwin.

Veatch, R.M. 1981. *A Theory of Medical Ethics*. New York: Basic Books.

Vincent, R.J. 1974. *Nonintervention and International Order*. Princeton, NJ: Princeton University Press.

Waldron, Jeremy. 1981. A right to do wrong. *Ethics*, 92, 1, 21–40.

Walzer, Michael. 1974. World War II: Why was this war different? In Marshall Cohen, Thomas Nagel and Thomas Scanlon (eds.): *War and Moral Responsibility*. Princeton, NJ: Princeton University Press.

Walzer, Michael. 1977. *Just and Unjust Wars*. Harmondsworth: Penguin.

Walzer, Michael. 1980. The moral standing of states. *Philosophy and Public Affairs*, 9, 3, 209–229.

Warnock, G.J. 1971. *The Object of Morality*. London: Methuen.

Wasserstrom, Richard. 1971. On the morality of war: Preliminary inquiry. In James Rachels (ed.): *Moral Problems*. New York: Harper & Row.

Williams, Bernard. 1985. *Ethics and the Limits of Philosophy*. London: Fontana Press.

Williams, Bernard. 1985a. Which slopes are slippery? In Michael Lockwood (ed.): *Moral Dilemmas in Modern Medicine*. Oxford: Oxford University Press.

Wolf, Susan. 1992. Two levels of pluralism. *Ethics*, 102, 4, 785–798.

Wolfers, Arnold. 1962. Statesmanship and moral choice. In *Discord and Collaboration. Essays on International Politics*. Baltimore: Johns Hopkins University Press.

Index

absolute priority principle, 43–45, 50, 53, 66
Acheson, Dean, 64
aggression: lethal, 79–82, 85, 119; political, 82–95, 119–120
Anscombe, Elizabeth, 123–124
appeasement, 120–121, 143n35
Aquinas, Thomas, 74–75, 89
Aristotle, 68
Augustine, 68–69
Austin, John, 72

Barry, Brian, 37, 40
Beitz, Charles, 45
Benn, S.I., 35
Blum, Yehuda, 121
Bluth, Christopher, 143n36
Britain (and the Hungarian nationalist revolt), 131–132
Brownlie, Ian, 126–127, 132–133
Bull, Hedley, 71
Burnham, James, 111

Carr, E.H., 140n10
Cassese, Antonio, 100, 103, 106, 121
Churchill, Winston, 27
Claude, Inis, Jr., 69–70, 103–104, 123
Cohen, Marshall, 65
colonialism, 125
communitarian argument, 128–129
consequentialism, 12, 15, 16–19, 139n3; strong consequentialist principle, 16–17; weak consequentialist principle, 17, 87, 128
counterfinality argument, 75, 102
Covenant of the League of Nations, 97

D'Amato, Anthony A., 73
Dancy, Jonathan, 63
decision under ignorance, 65–66
de Gaulle, Charles, 140n13
democracy, 31, 36–39, 41–42
deontology, 14–15, 19
desert, 114
deterrence, 114–117
discrimination principle, 89–95
disproportionality argument, 86–88
Donnelly, Jack, 127, 143n40
double effect: doctrine of, 90–91
double standard: normative, 113, 117, 134
Downie, R.S., 59
Dummett, Michael, 93

Eden, Anthony, 55
Elbe, Joachim von, 70, 78, 104
Elster, Jon, 137
equivalence: thesis of, 44–45
Erasmus of Rotterdam, 87
euthanasia, 132–133
Evera, Stephen Van, 107

Fain, Haskel, 140n11
Falklands War, 143n36
Farer, Tom, 127
Ferry, Jules, 125
first-person behaviour: morality of, 44–45, 48–49, 53–58, 62–63, 66
Fishkin, James, 12, 57
Fleischer, Carl August, 121
Ford, John, 93
Franck, Thomas M., 105

Gailiani, Abbé, 108
Gentili, Alberico, 78
Glover, Jonathan, 141n22

Godwin, William, 32–33, 49, 139n6
Good, Robert C., 27
Govier, Trudy, 141n22, n23
Grotius, Hugo, 71, 78
Gulf War, 142n26

Hague Convention for the Pacific Settlement of International Disputes, 103
Hampshire, Stuart, 136–137
Hare, R.M., 18
harm, 13–15; causation of, 21–23; principle, 14, 17–18, 45, 50, 52–53, 89–90, 119, 139n5
Hart, H.L.A., 143n34
Hegel, Georg Wilhelm Friedrich, 140n10
Heyd, David, 57
Hinsley, F.H., 140n10, 142n29
Hiroshima, 91
Hobbes, Thomas, 80, 121–122
Hoffmann, Stanley, 27, 65
holy war, 69, 141n20
Howard, Michael, 141n19
Hume, David, 76, 116

impartiality, 18–19
impersonal duty, 18
indeterminacy (in moral argument), 21, 62–63, 66, 85–86, 94–95
indiscriminate warfare, 90
innocent victim (of harm), 51–53, 89–95
international law, 71–74, 98–109, 117, 121, 123–127, 132–138, 142n30
intervention, 126; humanitarian, 126–134, 143n40; reform, 133
irrelevance argument, 74–75, 101
Israel: and Arab states, 108–109; and PLO, 113–115

Jackson, Justice Robert, 121
Johnson, James Turner, 89, 141n20, 143n36
just war theory, 67–71, 78, 89–95, 102, 119–124, 127–132

Kagan, Shelly, 139n7, 140n12
Kavka, Gregory, 84, 120
Kellogg–Briand Pact, 98, 142n30
Kennan, George F., 11, 25–30, 36–40, 43, 128–129, 140n9, 141n16
Keylor, William, 143n35
Krasner, Stephen, 39
Krauthammer, Charles, 143n39

Lackey, Douglas, 106
Lauterpacht, Hersch, 67
Lichtenberg, Judith, 23
Lillich, Richard B., 143n38
Lipson, Leon, 73
Locke, John, 38, 81–85, 113–114
Luban, David, 125
Lyons, David, 134

McCoubrey, Hilaire, 99–100
McDouglas, Myres, 105–106
Machiavelli, Niccolò, 54–55
Mackie, J.L., 21–22
Malnes, Raino, 10, 108, 141n15, n21
Martens, Georg Friedrich von, 71
marxist theory, 137
Mavrodes, George I., 91–92
Meinecke, Friedrich, 54–55
Mill, John Stuart, 130–132
Montague, Philip, 113–114
Moore, John Norton, 127
moral argument, 20, 34, 56–57, 139n7. See also indeterminacy (in moral argument), normative argument
moral dilemma, 21, 63–64
moral point of view, 11–12, 139n1
Morgenthau, Hans J., 27, 58
Munich Conference, 120–121
Murphy, Jeffrie, 83–85

Nagel, Thomas, 46–49, 56, 60
Nardin, Terry, 71
Narveson, Jan, 122–123
Nasser, Gamal Abdul, 55

national interest, 26, 35–42, 46, 54, 60, 62–63, 65
national obligation, 29, 31–32, 42–44, 62
need, 122–125
Niemeyer, Gerhart, 73
non-equivalence, 62; moderate thesis of, 49, 56, 58–60; strong thesis of, 49–52; weak thesis of, 47–48, 53–54
non-violent defence, 141–142n24
normative argument, 136–138
Norway (and NATO), 42

O'Brien, William, 109, 114–115
offensive war, 119–134

pacifism, 81
pacta sunt servanda, 43
partiality, 19, 45, 62, 65–66, 88, 111
Pauline principle, 89
'peace of God', 89
Peloponnesian War, 115–116
personal relationship, 13
Pfaff, William, 140n13
positional duty, 29, 31, 34–35
preventive war, 109–113
professional duty, 30–31
promise, 30–35, 49
proportionality principle, 142n25

Quester, George, 107

Rachels, James, 114
raison d'état, 25–29, 43, 50, 53–54, 67
Ramsey, Paul, 69, 88
rationality, 54–56, 66
Rawls, John, 143n31
Realpolitik, see raison d'état
rectification (of past injustice), 120–121, 125
responsibility, 29
retaliation, 113–117
revisionist thesis, 105
right: human, 127; moral (definition), 143n33
risky policy, 64–66
role, 29–31
Roose, Frank De, 85
Ruston, Roger, 142n27

Scanlon, Thomas, 15–17, 139n4
Schlieffen, General von, 107
self-defence: anticipatory, 104–113; national, 79, 82; right of individual, 79–82; right of national, 84–95, 97–104, 110, 113–117, 119–129. See also deterrence, retaliation
Sher, George, 143n31
Sidgwick, Henry, 21, 140n8
Simmons, A. John, 29
Singer, Peter, 18
slippery slope argument, 77, 107–113, 133, 142n30
Smart, J.J.C., 15
Smith, Adam, 9, 141n17
sovereignty, 70–71
special obligation, 19, 30, 32
Sterling, Richard W., 27, 30, 65–66
Stone, Julius, 107
Suez crisis, 55
supererogation, 57–60

Teichman, Jenny, 82–83
thermonuclear weapons, 64
Thomson, Judith Jarvis, 81, 94
Thucydides, 115–116, 143n32
Trainor, Bernard E., 142n26
Trianosky, Gregory, 77
Truman, Harry, 91
trusteeship, 26, 47–60, 62–66, 111, 117
Tucker, Robert, 82

United Nations, 73, 123; Charter, 74, 98–100, 104–106, 127; Security Council, 114
United States (and the Soviet Union), 110–111
utilitarianism, 12, 15–16, 18–19, 139n3

vagueness argument, 76, 111–112, 116, 125
Vann, Gerald, 120–121
Vattel, Emmerich de, 100–104, 110, 142n28, n29
Veatch, R.M., 30
vicarious action: morality of, 44–45, 48–49,

53–56, 58, 63–64, 70–71
Victoria, Franciscus de, 70–71
Vincent, R.J., 143n40

Waldron, Jeremy, 243n33
Walzer, Michael, 92, 120–121, 128–129, 131–132
Warnock, G.J., 136
welfarism, 17
well-being, 16–17, 140n12
White, Nigel D., 99–100
Williams, Bernard, 12, 141n22
Wolfers, Arnold, 65, 108
Wolff, Christian, 142n28
World War II, 92